In Such Hard Times

In Such Hard Times

The Poetry of Wei Ying-wu

Translated by Red Pine

Copper Canyon Press
Port Townsend, Washington

Cover art: *Ten Views of My Ideal Hut*, by Lu Hung (fl. 720), detail, National Palace Museum, Taipei, Taiwan, Republic of China

Frontispiece: Statue of a T'ang dynasty official at an imperial grave mound on the Tuling Plateau near Wei Ying-wu's old home. Photo by Bill Porter.

Map by Molly O'Halloran

Copper Canyon Press is in residence at Fort Worden State Park in Port Townsend, Washington, under the auspices of Centrum. Centrum is a gathering place for artists and creative thinkers from around the world, students of all ages and backgrounds, and audiences seeking extraordinary cultural enrichment.

Acknowledgments: Work on this book would not have been undertaken or completed without a translation fellowship from the National Endowment for the Arts, a translation grant from the PEN American Center, as well as food stamps and energy assistance from the Department of Social and Health Services and Olympic Community Action Programs in Port Townsend, Washington. I am indebted to them all.

LIBRARY OF CONGRESS CATALOGING-IN-PUBLICATION DATA

Wei, Yingwu.
In such hard times: the poetry of Wei Ying-wu (737–791) / translated by Red Pine.
   p. cm.
Poems in Chinese original and English translation.
ISBN 978-1-55659-279-9 (pbk.: alk. paper)
1. Wei, Yingwu—Translations into English. 1. Red Pine, 1943– 11. Title.
PL2677.W43A2 2009
895.1´13—dc22

2009000677

COPPER CANYON PRESS
Post Office Box 271
Port Townsend, Washington 98368
www.coppercanyonpress.org

for Tim Duke, Nic Gould, and Kim Stallings

I still have some solstice wine left...
and I know you have an old cart.
                              —WEI YING-WU

Contents

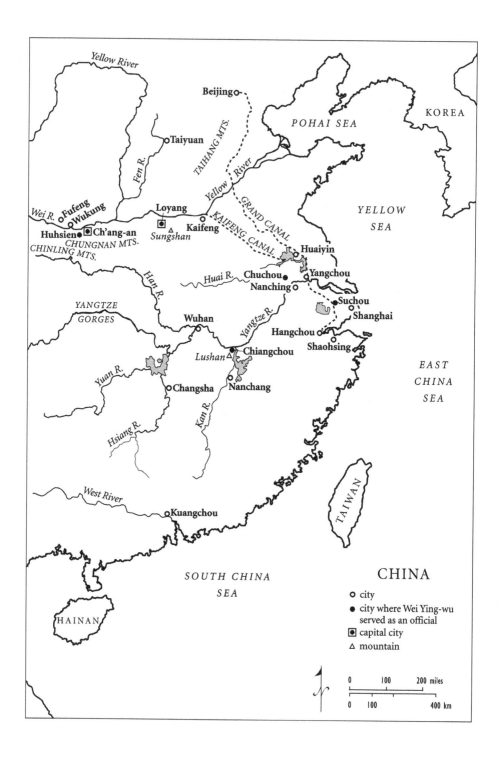

Yellow River

Beijing

POHAI SEA

KOREA

Taiyuan

TAIHANG MTS.

Fen R.

Yellow River

YELLOW
SEA

Wei R. Fufeng
Wukung

Loyang

GRAND CANAL

KAIFENG CANAL

Huhsien Ch'ang-an
CHUNGNAN MTS.
CHINLING MTS.

Kaifeng
Sungshan

Huaiyin

Huai R. Chuchou
Nanching

Yangchou

YANGTZE
GORGES

Han R.

Wuhan

Yangtze R.

Suchou
Shanghai

Hangchou

Shaohsing

EAST
CHINA
SEA

Yuan R.

Lushan
Chiangchou

Changsha
Nanchang

Kan R.

Hsiang R.

West River

Kuangchou

TAIWAN

SOUTH CHINA
SEA

CHINA

o city
● city where Wei Ying-wu
  served as an official
◉ capital city
△ mountain

HAINAN

0   100   200 miles

0   100   400 km

Translator's Preface

Wei Ying-wu (737–791) was one of China's greatest poets. But unless you are a student of traditional Chinese literature, chances are you have never heard of him. There are no volumes in English devoted to his poetry. Even in Chinese you have to look hard. I can count on one hand the books I have managed to find. Somehow Wei Ying-wu has slipped past unnoticed. But somebody liked his poetry and took the trouble to pass it down.

Less than thirty-five years after Wei Ying-wu died in Suchou, Pai Chu-yi (772–846) became magistrate of the same city. Pai was the most famous poet of his day and wrote, "Wei of Suchou leaves me speechless, the feeling in his poems is so pure and serene." Pai told his friends, "When it comes to five-character lines, Wei is in a class by himself." He liked Wei's poems so much he had some of them carved in stone. Pai wasn't alone in his estimation of Wei's poetry, but it wasn't until the Sung dynasty (960–1278) that Wei was finally recognized as one of the great literary figures of the T'ang dynasty (618–906).

In the Sung-dynasty poetry anthology *Chienchiashih* (*Poems of the Masters*), which Chinese schoolchildren have memorized for the past seven hundred years, only Tu Fu, Li Pai, Wang Wei, and Meng Hao-jan are represented by more poems among T'ang poets. And in the equally popular Ming-dynasty anthology *Tangshih Sanpaishou* (*Three Hundred Poems of the T'ang*), only Tu Fu, Li Pai, Wang Wei, Meng Hao-jan, and Li Shang-yin are given more entries. The Sung-dynasty neo-Confucian philosopher Chu Hsi (1130–1200) considered Wei Ying-wu's poetry superior even to Wang Wei's and Meng Hao-jan's. And yet, despite such appreciation and the inclusion of a few poems in anthologies, Wei has remained an enigma. He was, and still is, a poet's poet.

The reason critics give for Wei Ying-wu's lack of general recognition during his lifetime is that his limpid, serene style was not in vogue in the T'ang. In his chapter on Wei Ying-wu in *The Great Age of Chinese Poetry: The High T'ang*, Stephen Owen writes, "Wei's poetry was seen to possess a plainness that did not draw the reader by sensual attraction." In her essay "The Invisible Landscape of Wei Yingwu," Paula Varsano notes, "The essence of Wei Yingwu's poetry, like a faint and distant star, seems to dissolve under direct scrutiny." And in his entry on Wei Ying-wu in *The Indiana Companion to Traditional Chinese Literature*, Oscar Lee says, "He was not especially renowned, perhaps precisely because of the qualities which set him apart from contemporary tastes as exemplified by the clever, if unexceptional, verses of the *Ta-li shih ts'ai-tzu* [Ten Talents of the Ta-li Period]."

Besides the lack of ornate and clever language, there is something else missing in Wei's poetry. The poetry of the T'ang, whether coming out of the capital or the provinces, is laden with layers of allusion, allusions to all those people, places, and historical anecdotes an educated person should know and should delight in showing others he knows. It was one of the ways educated people displayed their credentials. Wei's poetry is bereft of all but the most basic allusions—there are far more, for example, in the poetry of his hermit contemporary, Han-shan.

Rather than trying to impress people with his erudition, Wei was more interested in drawing the reader into a landscape or a setting or a mood, especially the moods of seclusion and serenity. His poetry is also distinctive in its concern with the lot of ordinary people and not simply the educated elite. Finally, he was almost unique among major poets of his time in preferring old-style poetics: the five-character line as opposed to one of seven characters, and the relative absence of parallelism in adjacent lines in favor of a more natural flow of language.

But the apparent plainness that critics attributed to Wei's language is belied by the poems themselves, which are full of linguistic surprises. There was something else at work that kept his readers at a distance. In his youth, Wei seems to have developed a conscious disdain for the literary world. And rather than trying to compete with those for whom that world was the known universe, he fashioned a poetic style suited to his own sensibility, a style rooted more in the past than in the poetic tastes of the times, a style motivated and informed by a deep belief in the efficacy of the moral code that he represented as an emissary of the Son of Heaven. His fellow bureaucrats learned to mouth the teachings of Confucius. Wei lived them, or tried to. He was an unusual man, not just for his time but for any time.

The most repeated description of Wei states that he would not sit down without first sweeping the ground and lighting some incense. Despite sounding like a cliché, it gives us a sense of how he was perceived when he was alive. Those who knew him described Wei as taciturn and severe, even abrupt. The earliest descriptions say he had few desires and lived a life of aloof simplicity. This might have begun as an effort to distance himself from the excesses of his youth. But it became the persona by which he was known. It was a persona that also distanced him from others. By his own admission, he didn't do well in a crowd. He preferred the company of people he knew, those with whom he didn't have to put on airs.

But there was something else that served to widen the gap between Wei and the literary tastes of his times — and that was the sense of loss palpable in his poems. Even in his happy poems, his happiness has to rise above his sorrow to make itself felt. His life was lived in hard times. The Chinese still consider the T'ang their favorite dynasty, the high-water mark for much of what they admire most about their civilization. But it all came crashing down when Wei was eighteen. Of course, he was not alone in suffering through such times. But in comparing his poems to those of others, the shock clearly affected him more. And it did, I suspect, because the dynasty's history, his family's history, and his own history were so intertwined, their common thread being the loss of what had been and what could have been. Wei lived his life wondering what went wrong.

Since Wei's death, the details of that life have remained a mystery, except for what little his poems betrayed. In an effort to add something to my own account, I traveled to China in the fall of 2008. I was hoping at least to track down the location of Wei's old home. Maybe root around in the old garden. After arriving in Sian, I contacted a scholar I had met on an earlier visit. Although she wasn't able to help with my search, she passed me on to another scholar who passed me on to another scholar who directed me to an exhibition of grave epitaphs at Sian's Peilin, or Forest of Steles. Incredibly, the epitaphs on display were those of Wei Ying-wu, his wife, his son, and his son's wife. The four tombstones had only come to light the previous year when a pair of grave-robbers unearthed them in the Wei family cemetery (the exact location of which remains unknown) and sold them to Kao P'ing, a scholar who lived near where they were found and who taught at Sian's Northwestern University. Kao began studying the inscriptions and enlisted the help of another scholar in making a transcription of the epitaphs.

But once word got out about the find, officials at the Forest of Steles ordered police to confiscate the tombstones from Kao, who tried without success to defend his innocent intentions to preserve what have since been called "national treasures." The epitaphs were turned over to Ma Chi, a researcher at the Forest of Steles, who edited and published the epitaphs along with a summary of their contents in the fall of 2007 in a journal celebrating that organization's 920th anniversary. Since there might be others who share my interest in such matters, I have placed Wei Ying-wu's epitaph, as edited by Han Li-chou, at the back of this book, along with a photograph of the epitaph Wei wrote for his wife, which is the only known surviving example of his calligraphy. As the language used in such inscriptions is overly stylized when not obscure, I have limited myself to summarizing their contents in the account that follows.

Prior to the discovery of these epitaphs the only biographical information we had about Wei Ying-wu were character sketches consisting of nothing more than very tired clichés. Although a real biography will likely never be written, at least we have a few dates now and a better idea of the course of Wei's life.

Wei Ying-wu was born in 737 within a horseback commute of Ch'ang-an. Ch'ang-an was the biggest city in the ancient world, with two million residents, and it presided over an empire of another fifty to sixty million people during the most glorious period in Chinese history, namely the reign of Emperor Hsuan-tsung (r. 713–756). And the clan into which Wei was born was one of the most prestigious in all of China.

The Wei family had been sending its members to serve at court for generations. During the T'ang alone, it counted fourteen chief ministers. Wei Ying-wu's great-great-grandfather, Wei T'ing, served as Grand Councillor during the reign of Emperor T'ai-tsung (r. 626–649). And his great-grandfather, Wei Shih-chia, was Grand Councillor during the reign of Empress Wu Tse-t'ien (r. 690–705). But the clan also produced its share of prominent artists. In fact, Wei Ying-wu's father, Wei Luan, was better known as a painter than an official, as were his uncle Wei Chien and his cousin Wei Yen.

But times were changing. As with any society, some families were moving up and others were moving down. Wei's branch of the Wei clan was moving down. It wasn't a secret. The poet Han Yu (768–824) lamented the condition of the Wei family estate where Wei Ying-wu grew up. Wei never describes it, but I imagine a compound of a dozen or so one- and two-story, brick-walled, tile-roofed buildings large enough to house several generations: Wei Ying-wu's grandparents and parents, his older brother, and several uncles and their families. And each of the buildings would have had several small, enclosed courtyards where families raised their children and led their more private lives. There also would have been enough land outside the wall that surrounded the compound for an orchard and for the fields that supplied everyone with millet and wheat along with vegetables and fruit. There would have also been henhouses and pigsties and fishponds. And inside the wall there would have been an ornamental garden and a pavilion for watching the moon and drinking with friends and for enjoying the cool evenings during the hot summers. And there would also have been dozens of servants to do the cooking, the cleaning, and all the manual chores. And many of the farmers in the surrounding area would have been tenants on land owned by the Weis. In fact, the township of Weichu, where the family estate was located, still bears the clan's name. Yet it was an estate whose sources of income had diminished considerably by the time Wei Ying-wu was born. It was barely hanging on. In his poems, Wei is constantly looking back with nostalgia at the place where he grew up—but always making excuses why he couldn't return.

The family estate, whatever its condition during Wei's childhood, was located on the Tuling Plateau less than fifteen kilometers southeast of the capital and about ten kilometers north of the Chungnan Mountains. It would have been a fine place for rambling around on foot or horseback, as it had been for a thousand years. The plateau included a number of imperial grave mounds (from which comes the photograph in the frontispiece) and the remains of Yichun Palace, the country estate of Emperor Wu (r. 140–86 B.C.). And cutting through the plateau was the Huang Canal that fed the pleasure gardens of the Chuchiang Waterway at the southeast corner of Ch'ang-an. This wasn't simply farming country, though there were plenty of farmers. It was an area known for its estates and countryside excursions. This was where Wei Ying-wu grew up.

His epitaph says he was the third of three sons. In his poetry, Wei briefly mentions an older brother and an older sister, but his cousins were clearly his closest childhood companions, and he wrote dozens of poems to them throughout the years. He also took a great interest in his nephews and exchanged poems with them as well. But we never hear about Wei's father or grandfather—only sighs in their direction. Court politics were getting nasty toward the end of Hsuan-tsung's reign, and they got even nastier in its wake. Wei's family, it would seem, was too close to the tiger's mouth and suffered as a result.

Although his family's fortunes were on the wane, and although certain members might have suffered for political indiscretions, as the descendant of such an illustrious line Wei was invited to join the palace guard at the court of Emperor Hsuan-tsung in 751, when he was only fifteen—in Chinese reckoning a person is already a year old when they are born. Hsuan-tsung was devoted to the arts as well as to both physical and spiritual gratification. Convinced by his own excesses that he was living in a golden age, he paid scant attention to the administration of the realm of which he was the Son of Heaven. Wei Ying-wu entered the palace guard at the very end of this age of indulgence and later admitted he was guilty of his own excesses during his years in the emperor's entourage. But he was simply fitting in. Then it all ended.

In the winter of 755, General An Lu-shan rebelled in North China and led his army south. By the following summer, his forces were approaching Ch'ang-an from the east. The emperor fled west. Wei accompanied the royal entourage for a hundred kilometers, until it reached Fufeng. When the emperor turned south and continued over the Chinling Range into Szechuan, Wei stayed behind. Other branches of the Wei clan had holdings in the Fufeng-Wukung area, and Wei decided to weather the rebellion at a Buddhist temple in Wukung.

At least he did not have to weather the rebellion alone. In the fall of 756, Wei married a sixteen-year-old descendant of the Toba rulers of the Northern Wei dynasty. Her name was Yuan P'ing, and the sobriquet by which she was known was Fo-li: Buddha Power. It was a relationship that changed Wei's life. When imperial forces retook Ch'ang-an in the fall of 757, Wei and his bride returned to the capital, and he resolved to change his ways. He didn't have to wait long for an opportunity. Government forces also recaptured the dynasty's former eastern capital of Loyang that year, and despite his complete lack of experience or training, Wei was sent to assist officials in Hoyang County across the Yellow River from Loyang. No doubt, his wife's family played a part in this assignment, as this was where her clan was based. It was, however, a very minor and also a very short assignment. Rebel forces retook Loyang and the surrounding area in the fall of 759.

After a year or less in Hoyang, Wei and his wife returned to Ch'ang-an, and he enrolled in the Imperial College. This was the institution that trained young men for the higher echelons of government service. It was limited to five hundred students, all of whom were required to enter between the ages of fourteen and nineteen. Wei was twenty-three. But as the son of such an illustrious family, he was given an exemption.

However, his hereditary status also cut short his studies. Instead of completing the program, which normally lasted six years, and instead of sitting for the series of subsequent examinations that formed the normal path to government service, Wei bypassed the standard channels of advancement. The court needed warm bodies, bodies it could trust. In the fall of 763, Wei was given his first real assignment. The previous fall, imperial forces recaptured Loyang. Once the military had reestablished order in the city, Wei was appointed deputy magistrate of Loyang County, and off he went.

Government service was the only respectable career for someone of his background. Even though he did not go through the normal channels, it seemed to be the only career for which he was suited or, in fact, had any desire. But it was the source of lifelong disappointment. I think it was also one of the reasons his poetry was all but ignored during the T'ang. He was an aristocrat. Why should his fellow officials, men who had qualified for their posts via the examination system, treat him with anything but pro forma respect?

Also, Wei had his own standards. And they were often too high for the situations in which he found himself. In Loyang, he was especially upset by the government's reprisals against those who had sided or worked with the leaders of the rebellion, and he disapproved of the military's mistreatment of the common people. In the winter of 765, he was reported for ordering the beating of two military officers who overstepped their bounds. When he was reprimanded rather than supported by his superiors, he asked to resign. His request was granted, but not until the following year.

Instead of returning home, Wei remained in Loyang. That he did so could be taken as a comment on the condition of the family estate back on the Tuling Plateau. Or perhaps he was simply too embarrassed to go home. No doubt, he wanted to return as a success. But in truth he had a hard time accepting the dictates of government service. Wei, it would seem, never really got along with bureaucrats. Most of his close friends, the people to whom he wrote poems, were either family members or fellow aristocrats rather than successful exam candidates.

Unable to go home and without a salary, Wei was too poor to maintain the lifestyle of an official, even a retired one. He moved with his family—the first of two daughters would have been born about this time—into a Buddhist temple southeast of the city. Given his wife's devotion to the Dharma, and his own experience with monastic living during the An Lu-shan Rebellion, his choice was not as odd as it might seem. His usual explanation was that he was too poor. And perhaps he was. But he clearly got along better with monks than he did with bureaucrats. And he clearly had an interest in spiritual cultivation. Still, it was a cultivation that rarely surfaces in his poetry, except as a sigh that he had other responsibilities and following such cultivation to its conclusion would have to wait for old age—which was the standard Confucian response.

After several years of monastic living interrupted by occasional forays into Loyang, Wei finally had the opportunity to do some traveling, perhaps made possible by a friend of the family or some fellow official. In the fall of 769, he journeyed down the Grand Canal as far as the Yangtze port city of Yangchou. It was a good trip for him: his poems began to reflect a greater interest in the poetic moment than in simple narrative.

After several months Wei returned to Loyang and received his second major appointment in the spring of 770. He was made chief administrator for the Garrison Command of Honan Prefecture. Wei seems to have done better this time in accepting and carrying out his duties — or perhaps they were simply less onerous. But three years was as much as he could bear. In the spring of 773 he resigned again, citing a chronic illness, and he moved with his family — a second daughter was born in 771 — back into the Buddhist temple where he had stayed earlier.

But this time his stay was short. Less than a year later he returned to Ch'ang-an. His friend Li Huan had become chief magistrate of the capital and promised him a job. Wei returned in the spring of 774, and by summer Li Huan made good on his promise. He arranged for Wei to serve in the Metropolitan Labor Bureau and concurrently appointed him magistrate of Kaoling County north of Ch'ang-an. Although neither was a major post, they got him back to the capital after an absence of more than a decade.

These were Wei's happiest years: living in the capital near relatives and friends, enjoying a certain amount of honor as well as a regular income, and spending time with his family in a setting commensurate with his upbringing. At the beginning of 776 Wei's wife also gave birth to a son. But this happiest of times was brief. In the fall of that same year, his wife died of an unspecified illness. She had become Wei's confidant and companion and shared his love of poetry and calligraphy. Wei was heartbroken. The series of nineteen elegies he wrote in her memory are among his most moving poems. Once again, the theme that runs through his poems, that affects him most, is loss. He never remarried.

In the spring of 777, while he was still recovering from his wife's death, Wei was appointed magistrate of Huhsien, a county southwest of Ch'ang-an. It was another sinecure made possible by his friend Li Huan, who was still serving as chief magistrate of Ch'ang-an. Huhsien was a good place for Wei and sufficiently removed from the constant distractions of the capital. But this appointment lasted only two years. In the summer of 779 Li Huan was accused of wrongdoing and later executed. Due to his association with Li, Wei was stripped of his post and transferred to the small county of Leyang, east of Ch'ang-an. Rather than take up what he considered a demeaning assignment, Wei resigned, again claiming illness.

Once more Wei moved into a small monastery. This particular hermitage was located on the banks of the Feng River, between Huhsien and the capital. Owen notes, "The poems from these years begin to show the 'lofty grace and calm limpidity' for which Wei was best known in later ages." Indeed, these were Wei's best years as a poet, if only because he was not obstructed by government service and was actually able to follow the path of the poet-recluse, much like his hero, T'ao Yuan-ming. But neither could he resist the call of service. Early in the summer of 781, he was asked to serve as vice director of the Bureau of Judicial Review in the Department of State Affairs. He couldn't refuse, and he returned to the capital. He had been rehabilitated.

At about the same time, a number of provincial governors began rebelling against central government authority. Though Wei may not have enjoyed the highest favor of the court, it was at least assured of his loyalty. And from 782 to 790 he was sent to serve as magistrate of a series of important cities along the middle and lower reaches of the Yangtze.

His first such assignment was to Chuchou, not far from the port cities of Nanching and Yangchou, and he arrived there in the fall of 782. Despite the apparent prestige of such a post, Wei took it as a demotion. He had been sent to "the provinces." It was also the first time he was truly far from home — and far from his cousins and nephews. Still, he made the best of it. With nothing else to distract him, he wrote, and these were his most productive years as a poet. Since his post didn't require constant attention, he rambled around a great deal and often visited Yangchou. He also made friends with Buddhist monks and Taoist priests and maintained a correspondence with other poets.

When his term of office expired at the end of 784, he moved once more into a Buddhist temple just outside the city. This time he didn't have much choice. Li Hsi-lieh, the erstwhile governor of the western half of the Huai River watershed, had plundered Loyang in 783. And when the general who defeated Li didn't receive the reward he had hoped for, he sacked Ch'ang-an in 784. The emperor had to flee. The following year imperial forces retook the capital, but Wei still didn't return home. He stayed in Chuchou until the fall of 785, when he was appointed magistrate of Chiangchou (now Chiuchiang) in the middle reaches of the Yangtze.

Chiangchou was also at the foot of Lushan, one of the most scenic mountains in China, and near the old farmstead of his poet-hero T'ao Yuan-ming. However, from the moment he arrived Wei felt overwhelmed by the suffering of the people under his care. It was a constant source of anxiety, if not malaise, especially when he considered the suffering to be the result of government policies with which he did not agree. His poetry from this period seems forced, as if something else was on his mind, something he preferred not to talk about. Compared to his time in Chuchou or on the Feng River, these were not very productive years.

Fortunately, his term as magistrate of Chiangchou was only a two-year appointment. It came to an end in the summer of 787. But this time, Wei didn't move into a Buddhist monastery. He was recalled to Ch'ang-an to serve as director of a minor bureau in the Department of State Affairs. He was also enfeoffed as Baron of Fufeng, where he and his wife had weathered the An Lu-shan Rebellion, and he was given an entitlement equal to the tax revenue of 300 households. Wei had paid his dues in the provinces, and he once more had a chance to renew friendships back home and to revisit his past. But judging from the few poems he wrote during this period, it was a disappointing return.

In any case, it was a brief respite. In the winter of 788, he was sent off yet again, this time to serve as magistrate of Suchou, where he arrived the following spring. Unlike Chuchou and Chiangchou, Suchou was a prosperous city. It was a center of silk production and trade as well as a major rice-producing area. It was a good place to end up. A city full of gardens and waterways and no sign of refugees. Unfortunately, Wei was not able to enjoy it as he might have earlier. He was in poor health. He resigned sometime during the second half of 790 and moved into one last Buddhist temple, again just outside the city.

In addition to poor health, he also suffered from deteriorating eyesight, and he didn't write many poems during his two years in Suchou. The last datable poem was written in the spring of 791. He died later that year. His younger daughter, who was twenty-one, and his sixteen-year-old son accompanied his body back to Ch'ang-an, where he was given a temporary burial in the family cemetery on the Tuling Plateau that winter. The location given on the epitaph is "Wannien County, Fenghsi Township, Shaoling Plateau," the northeasternmost section of the Tuling Plateau southeast of Ch'ang-an. Five years later, in the winter of 796 when the divination charts were finally in agreement, he was reburied with his wife. His younger daughter died less than a month later. His son died in 809 at the age of thirty-four.

Except for Wei Ying-wu's epitaph, only recently unearthed, no one bothered to record any biographical information about him during the T'ang dynasty. Nor did the citizens of Suchou or anywhere else build a shrine in his honor. Someone, though, collected his poems. Perhaps it was one of his cousins or nephews, or perhaps his good friend Ch'iu Tan. It was Ch'iu who wrote Wei's epitaph, and in it he mentions that Wei's literary corpus included around six hundred titles. It was from this corpus that someone compiled the first edition of his poems, which has come down to us as the *Wei-su-chou-chi* (The Collected Works of Wei of Suchou).

In preparing my translations of Wei Ying-wu's poetry, I have relied primarily on the *Ssu-pu-pei-yao* version of this edition, which traces its ancestry back through dozens of previous editions to the earliest datable edition of Wei Ying-wu's poems, the one put together in 1056 by Wang Ch'in-ch'en. It was Wang who gave his book the title *Weisuchouchi*. In his short preface, Wang says he compiled his edition of 571 poems by using several earlier collections. But he does not mention the names of the compilers or the dates of compilation.

The reason we know about Wang's edition and not the earlier ones is that it had the good fortune of being compiled around the time that Wei's poetry was beginning to gain the notice of some of the country's most famous literary figures. It also had the good fortune of being compiled at the beginning of the printing revolution. In 1076, twenty years after it was compiled, a copy of Wang's handwritten edition found its way to the magistrate of Suchou, a man named Han To, who decided to honor his esteemed predecessor with a printed edition.

Although no copy of that first printed edition exists, we do have partial copies of subsequent *Weisuchouchi* editions as far back as the thirteenth century and complete copies from as early as the fourteenth. Among these editions, about the only differences are the odd character variation and deletion of a few poems. The total now stands at 561. The arrangement, though, hasn't changed.

The *Weisuchouchi* edition is ordered, by and large, according to the type of occasion that inspired the poems. Section One includes 21 poems of miscellaneous forms and 22 banquet poems; Sections Two and Three include 124 poems addressed to individuals; Section Four includes 66 poems seeing people off; Section Five includes 56 poems written in response to others and 7 poems on meeting people; Section Six includes 19 poems of recollections, 10 poems on travels, and 32 poems of lamentation; Section Seven includes 15 poems on looking into the distance and 58 poems on outings; Section Eight includes 89 poems on miscellaneous inspirations; and Sections Nine and Ten include 42 songs and ballads. The compiler, and I assume it was Wang Ch'in-ch'en, if not Ch'iu Tan, also did his best to put the poems in each section in chronological order—although it's an order with which every commentator has not necessarily agreed, myself included. Finally, some editions also add as many as 31 poems culled from other collections, bringing Wei Ying-wu's total surviving poems to 592—assuming one accepts them all.

Readers might notice, in the list of section headings in the *Weisuchouchi* edition, that 253 or 45 percent of Wei Ying-wu's poems involve a poetic correspondence with other people. This was, in fact, the nature of poetry in China. Poetry was as much a social art as a personal one. And even personal poems were shared with friends. Of course, this was also why it was possible to collect a person's poems after their death. First go through their belongings, then contact their friends.

Although nearly 600 poems sounds like a lot, Wei, no doubt, wrote many more than that. If he wrote one poem a week between his twentieth birthday and his death at the age of fifty-five, he would have written 1,860 poems, assuming a full thirty-five years of creativity. But given the social context of poetry in China, one poem a week would suggest a very limited social life, even for Wei. In one poem reminiscing about his youth, Wei tells us that he and his friends rode around with satchels full of their latest work. But whatever he wrote in his youth has not survived—I can imagine a big bonfire at some point in his life. Considering the limited appreciation of his poetry when he was alive, I'm amazed so many poems were passed down to us. Obviously, we have his friends to thank for that.

In passing them on now to an English-reading public, I've limited myself to 175 poems, or about 30 percent of those in the *Weisuchouchi* edition. In addition to including as much background information as I thought relevant, I have also added the Chinese text as it appears in the *Ssupupeiyao* version of the *Weisuchouchi* edition (though I have made a few changes where that text is clearly in error). I have also indicated each poem's location in that edition at the end of each note, where the first number indicates the chapter and the second number and letter the page in that chapter. Finally, I've organized my selections according to the probable dates of composition and have omitted poems for which I was unwilling to hazard a guess. Although my selections do no more than outline the course of Wei's life, I hope they provide a starting point for other scholars and translators.

In producing these translations, I must mention my indebtedness to a handful of people who have devoted themselves to the work of this man who has remained a mystery for so long. Despite the high regard Chinese literary giants have had for his poetry, Wei Ying-wu has not enjoyed the broad and comprehensive studies and commentaries given to other T'ang poets of his stature. However, there are five fairly recent works that stand out and without which I would have been far less likely to understand as many of the poems as I did. These are *Meng-hao-jan wei-ying-wu shih-hsuan*, by Li Hsiao-sung, published in Hong Kong in 1983; *Wei-ying-wu-chi hsiao-chu*, by T'ao Min and Wang Yu-sheng, published in Shanghai in 1998; *Wei-su-chou-shih hsiao-chi*, by Juan T'ing-yu, published in Taipei in 2001; *Wei-ying-wu-shih-chi hsi-nien hsiao-chien*, by Sun Wang, published in Beijing in 2002; and *Wei-ying-wu-shih-hsien*, by T'ao Min and Wang Yu-sheng, published in Beijing in 2005 — the first and the last of these being in-depth commentaries on a selection of poems.

I should also mention the usefulness of Thomas Nielson's *A Concordance to the Poems of Wei Ying-wu*, published in San Francisco in 1976 and long out of print. I have also benefited from the insights into Wei's poetry expressed by Stephen Owen, Oscar Lee, and Paula Varsano. My thanks to all these scholars for clearing enough of the trail for me to make out the visible landscape of Wei Ying-wu's poetry. Wei Ying-wu is not only one of China's great poets, he is one of the world's great poets, and his work deserves to be better known. Alas, I wish I were better equipped to present something finer than what tea and bourbon have inspired.

Red Pine
Insects Astir, Year of the Ox
Port Townsend, Washington

In Such Hard Times

I

九日

今朝把酒復惆悵　憶在杜陵田舍時　明年九日知何處
世難還家未有期

Written in the fall of 756 in the Fufeng-Wukung area. After the sack of Ch'ang-an by the rebel army of An Lu-shan in 755, Wei Ying-wu took refuge in this area one hundred kilometers west of the capital. Fufeng was where the fleeing emperor stopped for a night on his way to Szechuan and also was where Wei left the royal entourage. In Wukung he weathered the rebellion. Wei was not even twenty but already writing in the guise of an old man. In Chinese, *chiu* (nine) is a homophone for *chiu* (old). In such divination systems as the *Yiching*, this was considered the ultimate *yang* number. Hence, on the ninth day of the ninth month men gathered and drank chrysanthemum-infused wine (the words for this flower and for wine

The Ninth

On this day of drink and depression
I think about life on our Tuling farm
where will I be on the Ninth next year
in such hard times I can't hope to go home

were also pronounced *chiu*) and wrote poems commiserating with one another about the approaching end of their *yang* years. Wei's ancestral estate where he and his cousins grew up was southeast of Ch'ang-an in the village of Choukuei, near the northern edge of the Tuling Plateau. During the T'ang, Choukuei was part of Wannien County. Here, Wei refers to his old home as a *t'ien-she* (farm-stead), but readers should imagine a landed estate that had fallen on hard times. Tu Fu's ancestral home was on the same plateau a bit farther west. (8/8a)

PART ONE

Loyang

(763–773) / 32 poems

廣德中洛陽作

生長太平日　不知太平歡
今還洛陽中　感此方苦酸
飲藥本攻病　毒腸翻自殘
王師涉河洛　玉石俱不完
時節屢遷斥　山河長鬱盤
蕭條孤煙絕　日入空城寒
塞劣乏高步　緝遺守微官
西懷咸陽道　蹢躅心不安

Written in the fall of 763 in Loyang shortly after Wei arrived to take up his post as deputy magistrate of Loyang County. Given his confidence in the government's reassertion of control, this must have occurred before Tibetan forces sacked Ch'ang-an in the tenth month of the same year. The medicine refers to the court's use of the nomad generals An Lu-shan and Shih Ming-yi to protect the country from other nomadic tribes. Their rebellion in 755 brought the dynasty to its knees. The medicine also refers to the use of Uighur forces to retake Loyang, which occurred in the tenth month of 762 and which involved considerable retribution against those who sided with the rebels. It was during this period (the Kuangte Period lasted from the middle of 763 until the end of 764) that Wei arrived. "Jade and stone" refer to rich and poor. It would have been an instance of lèse-majesté if the lame and incompetent referred to the emperor and his court. More likely Wei had in mind the coterie of military officers and wealthy gentry that reassumed de facto control over Loyang following the city's recapture,

Written in Loyang during the Kuangte Period

I grew up in a time of peace
but I don't know the joys of peace
returning to Loyang now
I feel its pain and distress
we swallowed medicine to attack a disease
then inside us it turned to poison
our royal forces are back on the plains
but jade and stone alike lie broken
even the seasons have been driven off
while mountains and rivers keep winding on
lone wisps of smoke make this place bleaker
and dusk in a deserted city is colder
the lame and incompetent take few noble steps
compassion is the lot of minor officials
I recall coming east on the Hsienyang Road
stumbling along with an uncertain heart

while he and his fellow midlevel officials dispensed what little justice was possible. And yet he, too, is not exactly sure-footed in his dispensing of compassion, as he stumbles through the landscape of this poem. Hsienyang was the ancient Ch'in-dynasty capital across the Wei River from Ch'ang-an. It no longer existed as a city, but one branch of the Wei clan had extensive holdings in the Hsienyang area, and perhaps it was from there that Wei began his journey. The road to Loyang, whether from Hsienyang or Ch'ang-an, ran along the southern shore of the Wei and Yellow rivers. The distance was about 400 kilometers and took about a week to travel on horseback, which would have been the normal mode of transport for an official along this route—the Yellow River was, and remains, essentially unnavigable, except for local ferries. Wei speaks here of returning to Loyang. In poem 138, he mentions his first, albeit minor, assignment as being in Hoyang (Menghsien) County, across the Yellow River and to the northwest of Loyang. (6/12a)

3

趨府候曉呈兩縣僚友

趨府不遑安　中宵出戶看　滿天星尚在　近壁燭仍殘

立馬頻驚曙　垂簾却避寒　可憐同官者　應悟下流難

Written in 764 in Loyang. The governments of Honan and Loyang counties were under the jurisdiction of Honan Prefecture, and the officials of both counties were expected to appear at the daily predawn audience of the prefect. The prefect's offices and those of the Honan County government were on the south side of the Lo River two kilometers apart, while the Loyang County offices, where Wei was serving as deputy magistrate, were on the north side, six kilometers away—hence, he arrived on horseback. Instead of a wooden rail, the Chinese used stone posts to hitch their horses. They also used, and still use, heavy woolen blankets to cover doorways and windows during the winter. Commentators are convinced "those below us" refer to officials at the lowest levels. But given Wei's lifelong sympathy for the people, I suggest it refers to the masses. (2/4b)

Hurrying to the Prefect's Dawn Audience: For My Colleagues in Two Counties

We hurry to the prefect's without pausing to rest
in the middle of the night we look out our doors
the sky is still full of stars
lanterns are flickering next door
we tie our horses and rush to wake the dawn
and lower the curtains to keep out the cold
my pitiful fellow officials
think of the hardships of those below us

4

酬豆盧倉曹題庫壁見示

掾局勞才子　新詩動洛川　運籌知決勝　聚米似論邊
宴罷常分騎　晨趨又比肩　莫嗟年鬢改　郎署定推先

Written in the spring of 765 in Loyang while Wei served as deputy magistrate. Tou-lu was one of the administrators in charge of the supply section at the Honan Prefecture offices in the southern part of Loyang, where the two men would have attended the daily predawn audience of the prefect. Nothing more is known about Tou-lu. The term *lang-shu* in the last line usually referred, during the T'ang, to the director of the Department of State Affairs in Ch'ang-an. (5/5a)

Written for All to See on the Supply Section Wall in Reply to
Supply Administrator Tou-lu

Your talents are wasted in a clerical office
your new poems send waves down the Lo
the plans you've made I know will succeed
stockpiling rice I presume for the border
after a banquet we ride different ways
then hurry at dawn to stand side by side
don't complain about disappearing years and hair
the director is sure to promote you

5

期盧嵩枉書稱日暮無馬不赴
以詩答

佳期不可失　終願枉衡門　南陌人猶度　西林日未昏
庭前空倚杖　花裏獨留罇　莫道無來駕　知君有短轅

Written in 765 in Loyang. Wei sent this poem to a fellow official who was also serving in Loyang and with whom he exchanged a number of poems over the years. South Street ran between the imperial palace's south wall and the Lo River Bridge that connected the two parts of the city. West Grove was presumably outside the city's west wall. Or perhaps this is a mistake. In other poems, Wei mentions outings in the city's East Grove. (5/3b)

Waiting for Lu Hao, Who Writes Saying He Can't Come Because the Day Is Late and He Has No Horse, I Send This Poem in Reply

Such a fine day shouldn't be missed
I hoped you would finally honor my door
South Street is still full of people
and West Grove isn't dark yet
but I lean on my staff by the gate in vain
and your cup waits alone in the garden
don't say you lack a conveyance
I know you have an old cart

6

同德寺閣集眺

芳節欲云晏　遊遨樂相從　高閣照丹霞　颻颻含遠風
寂寥氛氳廓　超忽神慮空　旭日霽皇州　岧嶤見兩宮
嵩少多秀色　羣山莫與崇　三川浩東注　瀍澗亦來同
陰陽降大和　宇宙得其中　舟車滿川陸　四國靡不通
舊堵今既茸　庶甿亦已豐　周覽思自奮　行當遇時邕

Written in the fall of 765. Even with the end of the An Lu-shan Rebellion in 759 and the final recapture of Loyang in 762, a great deal of the central plains remained in de facto rebellion. Still, things were certainly better, especially in the Loyang area, and parts of the empire were beginning to enjoy the peaceful times to which Wei refers, if only briefly. Hence, maybe it was a good time to do some traveling. The year after he wrote this poem, Wei resigned and took up residence in this temple, which was just outside the city's southeast gate on the Yi River. But here he is just visiting with friends. Loyang Palace and Shangyang

Looking Out Together from Tungte Temple Pagoda

The sweet season it seems is late
and the pleasure of outings together
from a balcony lit by red clouds
whipped by a distant wind
the mist of loneliness dissolves
as our far-reaching spirits consider the sky
daybreak over the imperial city
two palaces towering high
the sight of Sungshao's flowering form
unrivaled by surrounding peaks
three rivers surging eastward
joined by the Mo and the Chien
yin and *yang* are in harmony again
the universe has regained its mean
boats and carts fill rivers and roads
the four quarters are open to all
the ancient walls have been repaired
the people are prospering once more
wherever we look we feel the excitement
of traveling while the times are good

Palace were about three kilometers apart and would have been visible in the dis-
tance to the northwest. About fifty kilometers southeast of Tungte Temple rose
the westernmost ridges of Sungshan and its Shaoshih Peak (aka Sungshao). The
three rivers visible from the pagoda's upper stories would have included the Yel-
low River thirty kilometers north of Loyang, the Lo River, which cut the city in
two, and the Yi River, which flowed ten kilometers south of the Lo and joined it
several kilometers past the temple. The latter two were also joined by the Mo and
the Chien before they entered the Yellow. (7/4a)

7

燕李錄事

與君十五侍皇闈　曉拂爐煙上赤墀
花開漢苑經過處　雪下驪山沐浴時
近臣零落今誰在　仙駕飄颻不可期
此日相逢思舊日　一杯成喜亦成悲

Written in 765 in Loyang. Because of his family's long and illustrious service, Wei was invited to serve at court as a member of the imperial guard in 751, when he was only fifteen. The guard accompanied the emperor wherever he went and consisted of three hundred young men drawn mostly from such families as Wei's. The imperial audience began every day before dawn, and the steps leading to the throne were painted red. The Yichun Garden, first laid out in the Han dynasty (206 B.C.–A.D. 220), was at the southeast edge of the capital along the Chu-chiang Waterway and was a favorite resort of the emperor and his court in spring. Lishan was a spur of the Chungnan Mountains thirty kilometers northeast of Ch'ang-an. It was also the location of the hot springs where Emperor Hsuan-tsung (r. 712–756) often spent the winter months with his favorite concubine,

Entertaining Adjutant Li

When we were fifteen we both served at court
we climbed the red steps through incense at dawn
we toured the Han Garden in bloom
and bathed on Lishan in the snow
but the Immortal has flown and isn't expected back
his advisers are scattered assuming they're alive
meeting you today thinking about the past
one cup makes me happy the next one sad

Yang Kuei-fei. Hsuan-tsung died in 762 and is referred to here euphemistically as the "Immortal." According to Taoist hagiography, the perfected adept is usually carried off by cranes or a celestial carriage to join fellow immortals in the lands of bliss. The identity of Adjutant Li is not known, unless it's Wei's friend Li Tan, to whom Wei addressed a number of poems. Despite the personal and dynastic tragedies of the intervening twenty years, Wei has not been able to resolve his feelings about the decadence of his earlier life and of the imperial court's. But at least he is no longer under their thrall. In some editions, the fifth line (which I have transposed with the sixth line) reads: "his advisers have scattered but they're still alive." (1/6a)

8

示從子河南尉班并序

永泰中余任洛陽丞。以撲挟軍騎。時從子河南尉班亦
以剛直為政。俱見訟於居守。因詩示意府縣好我者豈
曠斯文。

拙直余恆守　公方爾所存　同占朱鳥刻　俱起小人言
立政思懸棒　謀身類觸藩　不能林下去　祇戀府廷恩

Written at the end of 765 in Loyang. Wei Pan was Wei Ying-wu's nephew and also a good friend of Tu Fu, who wrote a number of poems to him. The red bird is a group of constellations in the southern sky. Chinese astrologers ascribe a noble character but also great sensitivity and a tendency to anger to those born under its sign. In his capacity as deputy magistrate, Wei had two members of the palace army flogged for abusing and causing injury to the common people. Wei's nephew maintained a similar attitude in his own dealings with the military. Each was reported to his superiors and was awaiting the outcome of their investigation. The Regency was the representative office of the emperor, which would have been ultimately responsible for the actions of members of the palace army. (2/4a)

For My Nephew Wei Pan in the Office of the Honan County Government

Preface: During the Yungtai Period [765–766], while serving as deputy magistrate of Loyang County, I ordered some cavalry officers flogged. At the same time, my nephew, Wei Pan, commandant of Honan County, was also strict in his administration of the law. Hence, we were both reported to the Regency. Since poetry reflects one's feelings, how could our friends in the prefecture and county governments find these words without merit?

A blundering directness is what I maintain
an impartial honesty is what you preserve
both of us suffering from the red-bird sign
we inspired the talk of small-minded people
worrying about threats while establishing order
we got tangled up trying to make a living
we can't run off to the hills
we can only hope for the prefect's mercy

9

任洛陽丞請告

方鑿不受圓　直木不為輪　揆材各有用　反性生苦辛

折腰非吾事　飲水非吾貧　休告臥空館　養病絕囂塵

遊魚自成族　野鳥亦有羣　家園杜陵下　千歲心氛氳

天晴嵩山高　雪後河洛春　喬木猶未芳　百草日已新

著書復何為　當去東皋耘

Written in the early spring of 766 in Loyang. The square hole and straight board refer to the poet—or perhaps the poet and his nephew. After Wei was accused of overstepping his authority, in having officers of the palace army flogged for causing injury to people in his jurisdiction, he was reported to the prefect and also to the regent. Wei refused to show remorse or make excuses and resigned out of protest. Technically, Wei was asking for a leave of absence. But according to bureaucratic protocol during the T'ang dynasty, any leave of absence that exceeded one hundred days was deemed permanent, which was what Wei intended in this case. Wei Ying-wu's family home was on the Tuling Plateau southeast of Ch'ang-an. But he was either too impoverished or too embarrassed to return. Sungshan was the central member of China's five sacred mountains and about sixty kilometers

Asking to Resign as Deputy Magistrate of Loyang

A square hole doesn't work with round pegs
a straight board can't serve as a wheel
materials all have their uses
denying our nature only makes us bitter
bending at the waist isn't my kind of job
surviving on soup isn't my kind of thrift
I'm retiring from life in a meaningless hall
I'll nurse my ills beyond the dust and noise
fishes swim free but still form schools
wild birds too form flocks
I'll be on Tuling in the family garden
perfumed by thoughts of a thousand years
or on Sungshan when the sky first clears
or between the two rivers after a spring snow
the flowering trees aren't yet in bloom
but new plants appear every day
why should I keep filling out ledgers
when I could be plowing those eastern fields

southeast of Loyang. It was also home to dozens of Buddhist and Taoist monasteries. The Lo River flowed through Loyang, and just north of Sungshan it joined the Huang Ho, or Yellow River. The area between the two rivers was a favorite place for outings of all kinds, especially on horseback. In his poem "The Return," T'ao Yuan-ming (365–427) said he was resigning his office and leaving to farm a small piece of land he had bought called Tungkao (East Paddy). T'ao's poetry and his decision to give up a government career for a life of simplicity were an abiding influence on Wei. But every time Wei resigned, whether for a few months or a few years, he allowed himself to be called back into service. As such service was the source of so much personal suffering, we can only wonder why. (8/4b)

10

任落陽丞答前長安田少府問

相逢且對酒　相問欲何如　數歲猶卑吏　家人笑著書

告歸應未得　榮宦又知疎　日日生春草　空令憶舊居

Written in the spring of 766 in Loyang. The identity of T'ien Wen is unknown. The "wine" of which Chinese poets speak so euphorically usually refers to rice wine with about the same kick as Japanese sake. Apparently Wei had to request a "leave of absence" several times before it was granted. (5/4a)

In Reply to District Defender of Ch'ang-an, T'ien Wen,
While Serving as Deputy Magistrate of Loyang

Finally meeting over wine
we asked about each other's plans
after several years I'm still a lackey
my family laughs at what I write
my requests for leave have been turned down
your fine career has known scorn too
every day brings more spring plants
but what good is thinking of home

II

贈李儋

絲桐本異質　音響合自然　吾觀造化意　二物相因緣
誤觸龍鳳嘯　靜聞寒夜泉　心神自安宅　煩慮頓可捐
何因知久要　絲白漆亦堅

Written in 767 in Loyang. The *ch'in*, or Chinese zither, consisted of a plank of
hollowed-out wood across the top of which were stretched five, and later seven,
silk strings on movable wooden bridges. The additional two strings at the top of
the *ch'in* simply repeat the lower two strings but an octave higher. The tuning is
still pentatonic. Silk strings have been replaced by those of longer-lasting steel.
The lightness of paulownia wood made it a favorite material among *ch'in* play-
ers, but cedar and other woods were also used. The *ch'in* was a constant compan-
ion of scholars and officials, like a cowboy's harmonica—though it did require
an attendant to carry it around. But then scholars and officials always seemed to

For Li Tan

Silk and paulownia are worlds apart
but their sounds combine so well
I can hear the meaning of creation
the connections between two things
in their resonance I mistake phoenixes and dragons
in their stillness a winter night stream
my mind and spirit feel at peace
cares and troubles are suddenly dispelled
what is it that calls old promises to mind
the purity of silk and durability of lacquer

have attendants. Here it provides the background music to this message to an old friend. And nothing in Chinese culture evoked friendship like the sound of a zither, for it recapitulated the meeting between Chung Ch'i and Po Ya when the two men became the model for all friendship of an intimate nature. Wei Ying-wu met Li Tan during his earlier service at court, and the two exchanged a number of poems. The virtues extolled here are the purity of the heart and the durability of friendship. In China the use of lacquer to preserve wood stretches back three thousand years. (2/4b)

12

早春對雪寄前殿中元侍御

掃雪開幽徑　端居望故人　猶殘臘月酒　更值早梅春

幾日東城陌　何時曲水濱　閒閑且共賞　莫待繡衣新

Written in the spring of 768 in Loyang while Wei was living in retirement in the suburbs southeast of Loyang at Tungte Temple. It was a spring tradition to go into the suburbs to find the first plum blossoms and to gather with friends along a winding stream, to take turns drinking from a jug placed on a floating raft and adding a line to communally written poems. It was also a custom to have new clothes made for spring. (2/5a)

Facing Snow in Early Spring: To Former Palace Censor Yuan

I swept the snow from my secluded path
living retired I look for old friends
I still have some solstice wine left
and plum blossoms are early this spring
how long shall we wander outside the east wall
and which day along that winding stream
take some time off and spend it on pleasure
don't wait until you're wearing new robes

13

假中枉盧二十二書
示稱臥疾兼訝李二
久不訪問以詩答
書因以戲李二

微官何事勞趨走　服藥閑眠養不才
花裏碁盤憎鳥汙　枕邊書卷訝風開
故人問訊緣同病　芳月相思阻一盃
應笑王戎成俗物　遙持塵尾獨徘徊

Written in the late spring of 768 in Loyang while on a permanent leave of absence. Lu Twenty-two was possibly Lu Hao or Lu Keng. Both men were serving in Loyang around this time. Li Two refers to Li Huan, whom Wei mentions elsewhere. In the first four lines, Wei is referring to himself. The "old friend" in line five refers to Lu Twenty-two, to whom Wei is replying in verse. In comparing Li Two to Wang Jung, Wei was referring to a story about the Seven Worthies of the Bamboo Grove. Once Juan Chi, the most famous member of this group, chided Wang Jung for joining them late while they were all drinking: "Here comes that

On a Leave of Absence, I Receive Word from Lu Twenty-two,
Who Claims He Is Ill in Bed and Surprised Li Two Hasn't
Visited in Such a Long Time. I Reply with a Poem and
Poke Fun at Li Two

Why did this minor official exhaust himself running errands
medicine and naps won't restore his talents
playing chess in the garden he complains about bird shit
reading books in bed he yells at the wind
an old friend inquires because he has the same illness
thinking of him this spring I lift up my cup
but I have to laugh at that vulgar Wang Jung
if I had a fly whisk I'd wave it from here

vulgar thing again to spoil our mood," to which Wang replied, "You mean your mood is something that can be spoiled?" (*Shih-shuo-hsin-yu: A New Account of Tales of the World:* 25.4) Wang was known for ignoring the dictates of membership in a group known for its cultivation of "doing nothing" and immersed himself in the accumulation of wealth. The fly whisk was used by the Seven Worthies and other intellectuals of the third century to make a point during their discussions of Taoist philosophy. It was later used by Buddhist monks for the same purpose and eventually became an abbot's symbol of authority. (5/4a)

14

答李澣三首

孤客逢春暮　緘情寄舊遊　海隅人使遠　書到洛陽秋

馬卿猶有壁　漁父自無家　想子今何處　扁舟隱荻花

林中觀易罷　溪上對鷗閑　楚俗饒辭客　何人最往還

Written in Loyang in the fall of 769, when Wei was living in retirement at Tungte Temple. Li Huan was on some unspecified assignment in the Yangtze watershed at the time. Eventually, Li became prefect of Ch'ang-an and arranged for Wei to return to the capital and to be appointed to the Department of State. Wei is replying to one or more poems from his friend. Hence, the references.

Ma-ch'ing was the personal name of the poet Ssu-ma Hsiang-ju (179–117 B.C.), who was so poor at one point all he owned was an empty hut. The fisherman is a standard reference to those who live a secluded life. In *Chuangtzu: 31*, Confucius meets a fisherman he considers a sage, and the fisherman, having imparted as much as he thought Confucius capable of understanding, rows off and disappears into the rushes.

In Reply to Li Huan

THREE POEMS

A lonesome guest encountering the end of spring
you sent a heartfelt account of our outings
from your distant post at the edge of the sea
your letter reached Loyang in fall

Ma-ch'ing still had his walls
that fisherman though was homeless
I wonder where you are today
in your little boat hidden among flowering reeds

I don't read the *Yiching* in the woods anymore
I drift with the gulls by the stream
among the singers of the ways of Ch'u
to whom do you most often turn

The *Yiching*, or *Book of Changes*, is an ancient divination manual and is studied by those intent on understanding the workings of *yin* and *yang* in order to achieve success in some endeavor. The seagull reference is to a story in *Liehtzu* in which seagulls react to those who try to catch them. Clearly, Wei Ying-wu has given up trying to catch anything. Among the poets most often associated with the Yangtze watershed (the land of the ancient state of Ch'u) were Ch'u Yuan (340–278 B.C.), who could not bear not to serve at court and committed suicide when his state was conquered, and T'ao Yuan-ming (365–427), who was only too happy to give up his government career. (5/4b)

15

自鞏洛舟行入黃河
卽事寄府縣僚友

夾水蒼山路向東　東南山豁大河通
寒樹依微遠天外　夕陽明滅亂流中
孤村幾歲臨伊岸　一鴈初晴下朔風
為報洛橋遊宦侶　扁舟不繫與心同

Written in the fall of 769, when Wei left Loyang for Yangchou. The comment in line five suggests that he is leaving via the Yi River and that this was where Tungte Temple, where he lived for several years after resigning his post, was located. The Yi comes from the south and flows into the Lo east of Loyang in Kunghsien County, after which their combined waters then flow into the Yellow River—here called the Great River. The sacred peaks of Sungshan are southeast of Loyang and force the east-flowing Lo into the Yellow. The wild goose, mail carrier for those separated by space, is being called on here to take Wei's poem to his colleagues. The wind on which it flies is the wind of autumn. The Loyang

32

Going Down the Lo by Boat from Kunghsien into the Yellow River: To My Colleagues in the Prefecture and County Governments

The narrow water the green hills and the road lead east
the peaks to the southeast make way for the Great River
leafless trees are indistinct on the far horizon
evening light shimmers and sinks in the flood
how long have I lived in this village on the Yi
the sky clears and a lone goose lands with the North Wind
my dear itinerant colleagues back at Loyang Bridge
my little boat is loose and with it is my heart

Bridge was built across the Lo River at the beginning of the seventh century and connected the city and county of Loyang on the north shore with Honan County on the south shore. Officials had to cross it on their way to and from the various government agencies distributed on both sides of the river. The Yellow River's constantly changing underwater sandbars made it a difficult river to navigate. Hence, from Loyang the normal route was to leave the Yellow at Kaifeng, then to go down the Kaifeng Canal to the Huai River and then the Grand Canal to the Yangtze. (2/5b)

16

淮上遇洛陽李主簿

結茅臨古渡　臥見長淮流　窗裏人將老　門前樹已秋
寒山獨過鴈　暮雨遠來舟　日夕逢歸客　那能忘舊遊

On the way to Kuangling (Yangchou) in the fall of 769, Wei wrote this in Huaiyin, where the Huai River and the Grand Canal intersect. Secretary Li is Li Huan, who previously served as the third-ranking official in Loyang, while Wei served as that county's second-ranking official. Li is between assignments. (5/14b)

Meeting Secretary Li of Loyang on the Huai River

You built your hut overlooking an ancient ferry
from your bed you watch the Huai flow by
the person in the window is looking older
the tree outside the door is already yellow
a lone goose flies past the desolate hills
a boat from far away arrives with the evening rain
day and night meeting travelers here
how can you forget our old rambles

17

初發揚子寄元大校書

悽悽去親愛　泛泛入煙霧　歸棹洛陽人　殘鍾廣陵樹

今朝此為別　何處還相遇　世事波上舟　沿洄安得住

Written in the winter of 769 on the Grand Canal. Wei was on his way back to Loyang after spending several months in the Yangchou area. Yangchou, or Kuangling, is located where the Grand Canal intersects the Yangtze. It is this last stretch of the river, from Yangchou to the sea, that locals call the Yangtze. The rest of the river is called the Changchiang, or Long River. The normal route by water from Yangchou to Loyang was via the Grand Canal, the Huai River, the Kaifeng Canal, the Yellow River, and finally the Lo River and took about a month. The man Wei leaves behind was a relative to whom he addressed other poems. His title indicates he was employed to ensure the accuracy of documents that originated in the prefecture in which he worked, which was most likely Kuangling. (2/6a)

Leaving the Yangtze: To Secretary Yuan Ta

With a sigh I left someone dear
and floated off into the mist and fog
with oars bent for Loyang
and Kuangling's bells and treeline fading
this morning when we said goodbye
we wondered where we would next meet
in a world like a boat on the waves
rising and falling with no shore in sight

18

和李二主簿寄淮上慕毋三

滿城憐傲吏　終日賦新詩　請報淮陰客　春帆浪作期

Written in the spring of 770 in Loyang. Li Two refers to Li Huan. Li was serving as secretary in the Loyang County government when Wei was deputy magistrate. Ch'i-wu Three (Ch'i-wu Ts'an) exchanged poems with a number of prominent poets, including Wang Wei. Ch'i-wu was serving in Huaiyin, where the Huai River intersects the Grand Canal. Writing poems at the beginning of the year was considered de rigueur among officials. For the last line, several meanings come to mind: the boats are bearing newly "rusticated" officials, or they're simply full of new poems from the capital. (3/11b)

Following Secretary Li Two's Rhyme: To Ch'i-wu Three on the Huai

The city is lousy with overbearing officials
writing new poems all day
tell our friends in Huaiyin
expect a wave of sails this spring

19

送元倉曹歸廣陵

官閑得去住　告別戀音徽　舊國應無業　他鄉到是歸

楚山明月滿　淮甸夜鍾微　何處孤舟泊　遙遙心曲違

Written in 770 in Loyang. Shortly after returning from his trip to Kuangling, Wei was appointed chief administrator in the Honan Prefecture Garrison Command. The quartermaster was in charge of provisions for government offices at various levels. Quartermaster Yuan, whose identity remains unknown, was leaving Loyang by boat for Kuangling, which was the old name for the city of Yangchou. The city was in an area that was once part of the state of Ch'u, and it served as the administrative center for the southern half of the Huai River watershed. During the T'ang dynasty, Buddhist temples rang their bells at midnight to remind people of impermanence: the end of one day and the beginning of another. (4/5a)

Seeing Off Quartermaster Yuan Returning to Kuangling

With office work slack I can slip away
we like our goodbyes sweet
there's nothing left where you grew up
you're going home to another place
the full moon above the mountains of Ch'u
the midnight bell in the land of Huai
where will your lone boat anchor
it's so far my heart turns away

20

李五席送李主簿歸西臺

請告嚴程盡　西歸道路寒　欲陪鷹隼集　猶戀鶺鴒單
洛邑人全少　嵩高雪尚殘　滿臺誰不故　報我在微官

Written in the winter of 770 in Loyang. This is an odd poem, written about some-
one seeing off another person. The person leaving was Li Huan, who earlier had
served as secretary in the Loyang County government and who now was return-
ing to Ch'ang-an to serve in the central government. Li Wu-hsi was Li Huan's
brother—hence the reference to the pied wagtail, a bird known for its love of
siblings. The Western Terrace is a euphemism for the Imperial Censorate, one of
the highest offices in the central government and the office to which Li Huan has
been appointed. Its equivalent office in Loyang was called the Eastern Terrace.
After requesting a leave of absence, officials had to wait one hundred days before
it was recognized as tantamount to a resignation. Sungshan was China's central
sacred mountain and about sixty kilometers southeast of Loyang. (4/3b)

On Li Wu-hsi Seeing Off Secretary Li to the Western Terrace

His leave of absence was finally over
even if the road leading west was freezing
he wanted to join the circling hawks
and left his loving wagtail alone
but families in Loyang seldom stay whole
even the snow on Sungshan is melting
he'll soon know everyone at court
and tell them about his junior-official friends

21

賦得鼎門送盧耿赴任

名因定鼎地　門對鼇龍山　水北樓臺近　城南車馬還

稍開芳野靜　欲掩暮鍾閑　去此無嗟屈　前賢尚抱關

Written in the spring of 771 in Loyang. To cast and set up a tripod was tantamount to establishing one's rule over an area or to founding a dynasty. This gate
was located on the south side of Loyang, and it faced the road that led past Lungmen (Dragon Gate), where hundreds of buddhas and accompanying deities were
carved. The river to the north would be the Lo, which flowed through the city.
City gates were closed at sunset and opened at dawn. Lu Keng served together
with Wei earlier in Loyang, but here he heads to some unspecified post whose
gate will require his protection, if only figuratively. Most commentators suggest
Kaifeng, to which the last line refers indirectly, as a famous official of ancient
times once gave up his life guarding the gate of that city. In the T'ang, Kaifeng
was considered the gateway to Loyang, since it marked the terminus of the canal
that connected it with the Grand Canal. But if Lu is heading for Kaifeng from
Tripod gate, he's heading in the wrong direction. (4/5b)

On Tripod Gate, While Seeing Off Lu Keng to His Next Assignment

The name comes from where a tripod was placed
the gate looks toward the dragon carving hills
towers and terraces line the river to the north
carts and horses enter from the south
the countryside is hushed when it opens
the evening bell is done when it closes
don't sigh in complaint as you depart
earlier worthies esteemed guarding gates

22

經少林精舍寄都邑親友

息駕依松嶺　高閣一攀緣　前瞻路已窮　既詣喜更延
出巘聽萬籟　入林濯幽泉　鳴鍾生道心　暮磬空雲煙
獨往雖暫適　多累終見牽　方思結茅地　歸息期暮年

Written in 771, while Wei visited the sacred mountain of Sungshan southeast of Loyang. Shaolin Temple was built in the fifth century for a monk from India named Buddha and was located in a high mountain basin at the foot of Sungshan's Shaoshih Peak. The trail from the temple to the top went right by the cave where Bodhidharma spent nine years in meditation. The chime to which Wei refers was used in Zen monasteries to mark the end of a meditation period. Although Wei sees through the illusory nature of his attachments, he can't let go. (2/6a)

Passing Shaolin Hermitage: To Friends in the Capital

I reined in my horse below a pine ridge
and hiked to the lookout on top
the trail appeared impassable as I started out
but once I arrived I wished it were longer
from the summit I heard a chorus of winds
in the woods I bathed in a secluded stream
the sound of a bell roused me on the Way
the evening chime cleared the clouds and mist
though my visit was brief
I finally saw what caused my troubles
but when I thought about building a hut
I knew it would have to wait for old age

23

送張侍御祕書江左觀省

莫歎都門路　歸無駟馬車　繡衣猶在篋　芸閣已觀書
沃野收紅稻　長江釣白魚　晨湌亦可薦　名利欲何如

Written in 771 in Loyang. The friend Wei is seeing off has requested and been given a leave of absence to care for his parents. Hence, his official robes are packed away, as are his favorite books. In short, he isn't planning to come back soon—but he is planning to come back. Chiangtso was another name for the area south of the last stretch of the Yangtze, between Nanching and the East China Sea. Brocade robes were required for attendance at court, with the color dependent on the office of the wearer. Rue was burned to keep insects away

Seeing Off Censor Chang of the Palace Library Leaving for Chiangtso to Care for His Parents

Don't sigh about the road beyond the city gate
or that you won't be coming back in a carriage
your brocade robes are there in your trunk
along with your books from rue-scented halls
with red rice grown in a well-watered land
and whitefish fresh from the Yangtze
your breakfasts can also be offerings
what good is longing for fortune and fame

from books and documents. Red rice was a variety that matured earlier and that allowed farmers in the milder Yangtze watershed to reap two harvests a year. The color refers to the husk and not the grain. The "whitefish" refer to a kind of perch, which were a seasonal delicacy of the lower Yangtze. The breakfasts here refer to meals prepared and served to one's parents. The cultivation of filial piety was considered the highest Confucian virtue, while fortune and fame were considered the goals of small-minded people. (4/5b)

24

賦得浮雲起離色送鄭述誠

遊子欲言去　浮雲那得知　偏能見行色　自是獨傷離

晚帶城遙暗　秋生峯尚奇　還因朔吹斷　疋馬與相隨

Written in the winter of 771 in Loyang. Nothing is known of the man to whom Wei writes this poem, although there is a couplet attributed to him in section 794 of the *Complete Poems of the T'ang*. Ironically, the couplet goes: "Thoughts of separation have no end or limit / just like rivers and mist in fall." (4/5b)

On Drifting Clouds and Signs of Separation While Seeing Off Cheng Shu-ch'eng

Before a wayfaring son says he's leaving
how do drifting clouds seem to know
they can see the signs of his journey
the pain of separation he feels
they darken the city from afar at dusk
they form strange peaks in fall
then the North Wind blows them away
with his horse following close behind

25

春中憶元二

雨歇萬井春　柔條已含綠　徘徊洛陽陌　悵恨杜陵曲
遊絲正高下　啼鳥還斷續　有酒今不同　思君瑩如玉

Written in the spring of 772 in Loyang. Yuan Er is apparently a relative, perhaps Yuan Hsi, to whom Wei wrote a number of poems. Wei grew up among the winding paths of the Tuling Plateau. (6/4a)

Remembering Yuan Er in Spring

The rain has stopped and it's spring in every courtyard
tender twigs are showing signs of green
I wander the streets of Loyang
sadly recalling the paths of Tuling
spiders are beginning to let out their silk
birds are back with their staccato calls
I have wine but it's not the same
it reminds me of your jade-like luster

26

遊龍門香山泉

山水本自佳　遊人已忘慮　碧泉更幽絕　賞愛不能去
潺湲寫幽磴　繚繞帶嘉樹　激轉忽殊流　歸泓又同注
羽觴自成玩　永日亦延趣　靈草有時香　仙源不知處
還當候圓月　攜手重遊寓

Written in the summer of 772 in Loyang. Lungmen, or Dragon Gate, was ten kilometers south of Loyang along the Yi River. Beginning in the fifth century, hundreds of buddhas and bodhisattvas were carved into the rock cliffs along its northern shore, and a dozen monasteries were built across the river on Hsiang-shan — Incense Mountain. The wings on the wine cup served as handles, and the "magic plants" refer to the mushrooms that were ingested as part of the Taoist diet designed to achieve immortality. They were considered most potent when the moon was full. (7/6a)

Visiting Hsiangshan Springs at Lungmen

The landscape is so lovely
visitors forget their cares
the jade springs so secluded
their delights are hard to leave
darkened ledges glistening with water
towering trees encircled with vines
the torrent divides into different streams
with eddies swirling beside the current
meanwhile I find a winged cup amusing
and the endless day prolongs my joy
magic plants smell sweet right now
the unexplored source of immortality
I think I'll wait until the moon is full
and come back for the night with a friend

27

贈王侍御

心同野鶴與塵遠　詩似冰壺見底清
府縣同趨昨日事　升沉不改故人情
上陽秋晚蕭蕭雨　洛水寒來夜夜聲
自歎猶為折腰吏　可憐驄馬路傍行

Written in the late fall or early winter of 772 in Loyang. The identity of his fellow official is unknown. Whoever he was, he worked in the offices of Loyang County, which were located on the north shore of the Lo River not far from Shangyang Palace, which overlooked the Lo. As his job title indicates, he was charged with reporting abuses by other officials. Wei, meanwhile, was working on the south side of the Lo in the offices of Honan Prefecture. Calico horses were designated for use by minor officials. (2/5a)

For Censor Wang

Your heart is like a wild crane far above the dust
your poems are as clear as a vase made of ice
lately we've been running around the prefecture and county
but all the ups and downs haven't changed our friendship
the swishing of the rain at Shangyang in late fall
the sounds of the night on the Lo in early winter
sadly I'm still a kowtowing official
a poor calico horse trotting along the roadside

28

休假日訪王侍御
不遇

九日驅馳一日閑　尋君不遇又空還
怪來詩思清人骨　門對寒流雪滿山

Written in the winter of 772 in Loyang. Officials had one day off every ten days.
On one such day, Wei visits his friend of the previous poem. He isn't home, but
at least Wei better understands where the man's poetry comes from. A censor was
in charge of reporting government, even imperial, abuses. (5/15a)

On My Day Off Visiting Censor Wang and Finding Him Gone

Nine days of being busy then a day of rest
I didn't find you home and came back disappointed
no wonder your poetry chills a person's bones
your door faces an icy stream and snow-covered hills

29

送鄭長源

少年一相見
飛轡河洛間
歡遊不知罷
中路忽言還
冷冷鵾絃哀
悄悄冬夜閑
丈夫雖耿介
遠別多苦顏
君行拜高堂
速駕難久攀
雞鳴儔侶發
朔雪滿河關
須臾在今夕
罇酌且循環

Written in the winter of 772 in Loyang. The hills north of Loyang between the Lo River and the Huang Ho, or Yellow River, were a popular place to go riding. Wei must have met Cheng when he came to Loyang in 763, when he was twenty-seven. Now he's thirty-six and looking back on his "youth." It's a matter of perspective. According to another poem Wei wrote to Cheng, the latter's hometown was in Chenchiang across from where the Grand Canal intersected the Yangtze. Wei's friend would normally be traveling by boat down the Lo and the Huang Ho and then down the Kaifeng and Grand canals as far as the Yangtze. But the Kaifeng Canal was at this time under the control of regional warlords who no longer accepted the court's authority. Hence, Wei's friend is taking the overland route. Manuals for the *ch'in*, or Chinese zither, use the names of animals, some real, some imaginary, to describe the sounds to be played on its silken strings. (4/6b)

Seeing Off Cheng Ch'ang-yuan

From the time we met in our youth
our bridles flashed between the two rivers
we've never tired of rambling
now without warning you're leaving
the plaintive cry of phoenix strings
the utter stillness of a winter night
despite a gentleman's resolve
the coming separation shows on our faces
you're traveling home to honor your parents
I can't hold back your fleet-footed steed
when the rooster crows you'll depart my friend
with winter snows still blocking the passes
our time tonight is so brief
fill your cup one more time

30

送洛陽韓丞東遊

仙鳥何飄颻　綠衣翠為襟　顧我差池羽　咬咬懷好音
徘徊洛陽中　遊戲清川潯　神交不在結　歡愛自中心
駕言忽徂征　雲路邈且深　朝遊尚同啄　夕息當異林
出餞宿東郊　列筵屬城陰　舉酒欲為樂　憂懷方沉沉

Written in the spring of 773 in Loyang. Seeing off a friend, Wei likens him to a parrot, the bird of immortals, while he takes the guise of a swallow, with its uneven tail feathers. His friend is apparently leaving on a diplomatic mission to the provinces east of Loyang that were controlled by officials who had become regional warlords and who no longer accepted the central government's authority. The use of a green robe was restricted to mid-level posts, while blue robes were limited to low-level officials. (4/6a)

Seeing Off Magistrate Han of Loyang on His Trip East

This bird of the immortals born for the wind
with turquoise lapels and robe of green
regards my feathers as peculiar
as I twitter away thinking I can sing
we flew back and forth across Loyang
amusing ourselves along crystal streams
friendship with the gods wasn't meant to be
but happiness filled our hearts
now you're leaving on a distant mission
on a long dark road through the clouds
but we can still drink and enjoy this day
and sleep tonight among different trees
I've paid for lodging east of the city
and spread out a feast in the shade of the wall
as I lift this wine and wish you well
the sadness I feel makes it seem heavy

31

假中對雨呈縣中僚友

卻足堪為笑　閑居夢杜陵　殘鸎知夏淺　社雨報年登
流麥非關忘　收書獨不能　自然憂曠職　緘此謝良朋

Written in the late spring of 773 in Loyang after Wei resigned due to illness. Ch'ueh K'o was a general of the first millennium B.C. known for his deformed feet. Wei suffered from a foot disease or malformation of some kind, which was the reason he gave for quitting his post. Being too poor to travel home to Tuling, he remained in Loyang at Tungte Temple—the same place he lived after resigning in 766. The Chinese oriole is associated with spring, and spring is almost over. Wei senses that his career in government service is also over—though it

On Leave and Watching the Rain: To My Colleagues in the County Government

With feet like Ch'ueh K'o's I get nothing but laughs
unemployed now I dream of Tuling
the last oriole knows little of summer
but a festival rain foretells a good harvest
my grain isn't gone because I wasn't looking
compiling records was something I couldn't do
of course I worry about quitting my post
I'd better stop here and thank my friends

would continue off and on for another twenty years. The spring festival honor-ing the Earth God was held forty-five days after February 5. Hence, this poem was written in late March. There was once a man so immersed in reading books that he didn't notice when a rainstorm blew away the grain he was drying in the sun. Officials were paid in grain, which they then exchanged for cash. Wei is no longer an official, but he feels compelled to stop short of voicing what might have been his real reasons for retiring. (2/4a)

32

同德寺雨後寄元侍御李博士

川上風雨來　須臾滿城闕
岧嶢青蓮界　蕭條孤興發
前山遽已淨　陰靄夜來歇
喬木生夏涼　流雲吐華月
嚴城自有限　一水非難越
相望曙何遠　高齋坐超忽

Written in the late summer of 773 in Loyang's southeastern outskirts at Tungte Temple. Loyang was often used as the eastern capital of the T'ang dynasty, while Ch'ang-an was the western capital. Hence, both were considered imperial cities. Loyang straddled both sides of the Lo River, which here brings a summer rainstorm. Flowering only after it rises above the mud, the lotus was a symbol of buddhahood and here stands for a Buddhist temple — especially a pagoda. The blue lotus was the rarest of all, and its petals were said to resemble the Buddha's eyes.

At Tungte Temple after a Rain: To Censor Yuan and Professor Li

Wind and rain come down the river
quickly enfolding the imperial city
the realm of towering blue lotuses
stands apart in the bleakness
the nearby hills are suddenly purified
the vapor disappears as the night arrives
tall trees cool the summer air
drifting clouds unveil a brocade moon
the Forbidden City has its restrictions
but a single river isn't that hard to cross
dawn is far off and already I'm waiting
in my lofty quarters in wistful reverie

As a summer rainstorm clears the air of dust, the poet thinks of friends in the city and wishes they could cross the Lo River and visit him. But the city gates were closed at sunset (after a huge drum was stuck 800 times — giving everyone within earshot plenty of time to get inside), and they remained closed until just before dawn. Wei uses the phrase *kao-chai* ("lofty quarters") so often in his poetry, it's hard to know if it's just a cliché for "fancy lodging" or whether it actually refers to a room, or set of rooms, on the second floor. Perhaps both. (2/6b)

33

庭樹忽已暗　故人何不來　祇應猒煩暑　永日坐霜臺

同德閣期元侍御李博士不至
各投贈二首

官榮多所繫　閑居亦儵期　高閣猶相望　青山欲暮時

These two linked poems were written in the late summer of 773, while Wei was living outside Loyang at Tungte Temple and recuperating from an illness or otherwise enjoying a temporary retirement. The office where Censor Yuan served was known as "the frost-covered terrace" because its work dealt with calling other officials to task and was not normally a welcome place to visit. Hence, the first poem is for Censor Yuan. The term *kao-ke* ("high structure") usually referred to a pagoda from which one could look out, but it also sometimes referred to the multistoried building common to most monasteries on whose upper floors were stored the Buddhist Canon and other sacred texts. The ridges that have lost the day's last light are those of Sungshan to the southeast of both Loyang and Tungte Temple. (2/7a)

After Waiting for Censor Yuan and Professor Li at Tungte
Temple, When Neither Arrives, I Send Each a Poem

The courtyard trees are suddenly dark
why didn't my old friend come
it must be because he hates the heat
and spends his days on a frost-covered terrace

The glory of office comes with its burdens
retired life too means less time together
I watched for you from the upper story
until the blue ridges were almost black

PART TWO

Ch'ang-an

(774–782) / 51 poems

34

陪元侍御春遊

何處醉春風　長安西復東　不因俱罷職　豈得此時同
貰酒宣平里　尋芳下苑中　往來楊柳陌　猶避昔年驄

Written in the spring of 774 in Ch'ang-an upon Wei's return to the capital. Wei and Yuan were relatives, though the nature of their relationship is unknown. They exchanged a number of poems while serving in Loyang and meet here again in Ch'ang-an. Looking for the first signs of spring was a popular pursuit of ancient China's leisure class. Hsuanping Quarter was southeast of the Forbidden City and just north of Hsiayuan Garden, which bordered the Chuchiang Waterway. Wei was living in Chaokuo Quarter between the two. The use of calico horses was restricted to minor officials, and here refer to the officials themselves. Dodging such horses goes back to an overbearing official named Huan Tien who rode through the capital without worrying whether he might knock someone down. Willow-lined paths may also refer to the lanes where brothels were located. Although Wei was back in Ch'ang-an with the expectation of an appointment, he clearly was still waiting. (7/6a)

Accompanying Censor Yuan on an Outing in Spring

Where is that drunken spring wind
west of Ch'ang-an or east
if we hadn't both resigned
we wouldn't be here together
in Hsuanping Quarter buying wine on credit
or looking for flowers in Hsiayuan Garden
coming and going on willow-lined paths
still dodging those calico horses of the past

35

送榆次林明府

無嗟千里遠　亦是宰王畿　策馬雨中去　逢人關外稀

邑傳榆石在　路遠晉山微　別思方蕭索　新秋一葉飛

Written in the fall of 774 in Ch'ang-an, not long after Wei was appointed as an administrator in the Metropolitan Labor Bureau. The identity of Magistrate Lin is unknown. The "royal realm" included all the land within a thousand *li* of the capital, and any assignment within this area was considered a sign of favor. Two *li* equaled one kilometer, and three *li* equaled a mile. Yutzu was the name of a prefecture just east of the garrison city of Taiyuan about 500 kilometers northeast of Ch'ang-an. It was once the capital of the ancient state of Chin and was known for a rock said to have advised its king, Wei Yu. (4/7a)

Seeing Off District Magistrate Lin to Yutzu

Don't sigh about living a thousand *li* from home
you'll still be within the royal realm
whip your horse on in the rain
fellow travelers are few beyond the passes
your post is known for the Rock of Yu
and the narrow road through the Mountains of Chin
as the bleakness of your departure settles
an early autumn leaf blows past

36

送汾城王主簿

少年初帶印　汾上又經過　芳草歸時徧　情人故郡多
禁鍾春雨細　宮樹野煙和　相望東橋別　微風起夕波

Written in the spring of 775 in Ch'ang-an. Officials carried their seal of office attached to their belts by a ribbon whose color depended on their status. Wei is seeing off his friend at the Pa River Bridge, which was eight kilometers northeast of the capital and where people saw off friends heading east. Wei's friend is returning to the county seat of Fencheng, known nowadays as Linfen, on the Fen River 400 kilometers northeast of Ch'ang-an. His title indicates that he will be serving under the deputy magistrate. Taming Palace was just inside the city wall of Ch'ang-an and ten kilometers southeast of the bridge, and adjacent to the palace were the forbidden precincts of the royal forest. The smoke is from burning the detritus of the previous year's harvest. (4/8a)

Seeing Off Secretary Wang to Fencheng

You've carried a seal since you were young
you've been up the Fen River before
sweet-smelling plants will be there to greet you
so will many old friends
the palace bell and spring rain are faint
the royal forest and farm smoke have merged
as I watch you head east from the bridge
a light wind stirs evening waves

37

送別覃孝廉

思親自當去　不第未蹉跎　家住青山下　門前芳草多

称歸通遠徼　巫峽注驚波　州舉年年事　還期復幾何

Written in 775 in Ch'ang-an. The man whom Wei sees off has taken and failed the
civil service exam in the capital and is now returning to his home in the middle
of the Yangtze's Three Gorges. Tzukuei was also Ch'u Yuan's hometown. Ch'u
Yuan (d. 278 B.C.) was China's first great poet and one who used various plants
in his poetry to represent the virtues and failings of his fellow officials. The route
from Ch'ang-an to Tzukuei required travelers to negotiate the Chinling Moun-
tains and then the Yangtze's Chutang and Wu gorges. Candidates who sat for the
exam in the capital first had to pass an exam at the provincial level. However, the
man Wei sees off was previously exempt from the provincial exam because of his
exceptional filial piety. (4/7b)

Seeing Off Candidate T'an

It's right to go care for your parents
but failing an exam doesn't make you a failure
your home is at the foot of blue mountains
outside your door are sweet-smelling plants
the road from Tzukuei may be long and narrow
and the currents of Wu Gorge alarming
but provincial exams are an annual event
it won't be long before you're back again

38

高陵書情寄三原盧少府

直方難為進　守此微賤班　開卷不及顧　沉埋案牘間
兵凶久相踐　徭賦豈得閑　促戚下可哀　寬政身致患
日夕思自退　出門望故山　君心儻如此　攜手相與還

Written in 775 while serving concurrently as labor administrator in the capital
and as magistrate of Kaoling County, thirty kilometers northeast of Ch'ang-an.
Both were minor posts. Wei's friend was serving in Sanyuan, the adjacent county
west of Kaoling. As a labor administrator, Wei was in charge of work gangs made
up of men and boys serving corvée, which required every family to supply a male
to work on state projects, such as roads and city walls. Even after the An Lu-
shan Rebellion was crushed in 759, warfare and banditry never really ceased.
The mountains to which Wei refers are the Chungnan Mountains thirty kilo-
meters south of Ch'ang-an, near his home and presumably Commandant Lu's
home as well. The phrase *hsiang-yu-huan* ("let's go back together") is from T'ao
Yuan-ming's poem "The Return," in which the fourth-century poet voices simi-
lar sentiments. (2/3b)

In Kaoling Describing My Feelings to Commandant Lu of Sanyuan

The straight and the square rarely advance
I'm serving in the stupidest of posts
I don't have time to open a book
buried beneath casework and records
the disaster of war has worn us all down
there's no vacation from corvée and taxes
the downtrodden masses need help
but compassionate measures only cause us trouble
I think of retiring day and night
from outside my door I can see the old mountains
if you feel the same
let's go back arm-in-arm together

39

登寶意寺上方舊遊

翠嶺香臺出半天　萬家煙樹滿晴川

諸僧近住不相識　坐聽微鍾記往年

Written in 775 while visiting a Buddhist temple eighty kilometers west of Ch'ang-an. In a note to this poem, Wei says this temple was near the town of Wukung and that he had stayed there in the past. The consensus is that this was where he lived while lying low during the first year or two of the An Lu-shan Rebellion (755–759). The temple was a former estate that became a Buddhist monastery in the second half of the seventh century, and perhaps the previous owners were connected with his family. The *shang-fang* (upper section) of a monastery was usually farther up the slope from the main set of buildings, sort of an annex that often developed from the huts of hermits. In this case, the slope was that of Wukungshan, the hill after which the town was named. The river here is the Wei (no relation). (7/4b)

*Climbing to the Upper Section of Paoyi Temple, Which I
Visited Before*

Jade ridges and incense-veiled terraces stretch halfway to heaven
ten thousand households and mist-covered trees line the clearing river
I don't know the monks because they're all new
but listening to the fading bell I recall that distant year

40

石鼓歌

周宣大獵兮岐之陽　刻石表功兮煒煌煌
石如皷形數止十　風雨缺訛苔蘚澀
今人濡紙脫其文　既擊既埽白黑分
忽開滿卷不可識　驚潛動蟄走云云
喘逶迤相糺錯　乃是宣王之臣史籀作
一書遺此天地間　精意長存世冥窒
秦家祖龍還刻石　碣石之罘李斯跡
世人好古猶共傳　持來比此殊縣隔

Written in 775 while visiting the Wukung-Fufeng area west of Ch'ang-an. At the beginning of the seventh century these stone drums were unearthed south of Mount Ch'i, not far from Fufeng. Mount Ch'i was the ancestral home of the rulers of the state of Ch'in who eventually united all of China in 221 B.C. The stones were inscribed with poems recounting the hunting expeditions of King Hsuan (r. 827–782 B.C.) of the Chou dynasty, in the calligraphy of his chief minister, Shih Liu. The consensus among scholars of the time was that they were carved during the First Emperor's reign, which ended in 209 B.C. The First Emperor left similar inscriptions on the slopes of Chiehshih in Hopei and Chihchung in Shantung, likewise recounting his own exploits, but in the calligraphy of his chief minister, Li Ssu. The Chinese consider calligraphy the greatest of all graphic arts and make copies of stone inscriptions by placing a slightly moist sheet of rice paper on the surface. Once the paper dries, it is then patted with an ink-infused cloth until it is blackened and the inscription appears in white relief. (9/5b)

Song of the Stone Drums

King Hsuan of Chou hunting south of Mount Ch'i
the artistry of the carving finely rendered
on drum-shaped stones ten in number
eroded by the weather half-eaten by moss
people today wet paper to make prints
patting and brushing until black and white become clear
but no one can read the whole scroll
as lines leap from hiding then vanish
swirl in circles then merge
the work of Prime Minister Shih Liu
who wrote and left this for the world to see
whose spirit has endured the oblivion of time
the Dragon Lord of Ch'in had stones carved too
on Chiehshih and Chihchung are the traces of Li Ssu
people love the ancients and honor their traditions
but looking at these stones how far off they seem

41

月夜會徐十一草堂

空齋無一事　岸幘故人期　暫輟觀書夜　還題翫月詩
遠鍾高枕後　清露卷簾時　暗覺新秋近　殘河欲曙遲

Written in the summer of 775 in Kaoling. Officials were required to have a head covering in place at all times, even when entertaining. But here, both men have put aside official decorum. The references to "the bell" and "a comfortable sleep" suggest proximity to a Buddhist temple. One of the dictates of the Buddhist regimen specifies avoiding *kao-chen* (comfortable bedding). Hence, Wei is poking fun at his friend's minor indulgence. The "vanishing river" is the Milky Way at daybreak. As magistrate, Wei would have been expected to be at work before dawn. (1/7a)

On a Moonlit Night Meeting at Hsu Eleven's Thatched Hut

In an empty study with nothing to do
you loosened your hat strings and waited for a friend
it wasn't a night for reading
but for writing poems about the moon
after listening to the bell and sleeping in comfort
we rolled up dew-covered blinds
and sensed another fall was near
while the fading river tried to hold off dawn

42

藍嶺精舍

石壁精舍高　排雲聊直上　佳遊愜始願　忘險得前賞
崖傾景方晦　谷轉川如掌　綠林含蕭條　飛閣起弘敞
道人上方至　深夜還獨往　日落羣山陰　天秋百泉響
所嗟累已成　安得長偃仰

Written in the fall of 775 while on a mission to Lantien, sixty kilometers southeast of Ch'ang-an. Lanling refers to a ridge of the Chungnan Mountains south of Lantien. Many hermits in this area still build their huts out of stone, which is more plentiful than wood. While Wei can't bring himself to give up the attraction of government service for the apparent loneliness of spiritual cultivation, he continues to be aware of his self-inflicted suffering. (7/11b)

Lanling Hermitage

Up high to a cloister of rock walls
I pushed aside clouds and climbed
a fine hike was what I hoped for
ignoring the dangers I reached my prize
but as light on the escarpment faded
and streams branched out like the lines in my hand
and the forests held nothing but loneliness
and the pinnacles disappeared into space
a man of the Way after reaching such heights
descended alone in the stillness of night
the mountain turned dark after sunset
a hundred springs echoed across the fall sky
my lamentable burdens reappeared intact
why can't I stay free of cares

43

采玉行

官府徵白丁　言采藍谿玉
絕嶺夜無家　深榛雨中宿
獨婦餉糧還　哀哀舍南哭

Written in the fall of 775 while on a mission to Lantien. The Lan River flowed north out of the Chungnan Mountains sixty-five kilometers southeast of Ch'ang-an and was famous for its jade, which was found along the river's banks but also mined in greater quantities along the cliffs near its upper reaches. Nowadays the same area is known for its uranium. As this wife returns from visiting her husband, she looks back toward the towering peaks immediately to the south, beyond which her husband is now living. The government had the power to conscript one able-bodied male from every family for labor or for war for indeterminate periods. Wei's duties in the Labor Bureau required him to visit projects involving such conscripts. It was obviously not a rewarding job. (10/4b)

Jade Diggers Ballad

The government drafts a common man
tells him to dig for Lan River jade
over the ridge nights away from home
he sleeps in thickets of thorns in the rain
his wife returns from taking him food
and sobs just south of their home

44

贈馮著

契闊仕兩京　念子亦飄蓬　方來屬追往　十載事不同

歲晏乃云至　微褐還未充　慘悽遊子情　風雪自關東

華觴發懽顏　嘉藻播清風　始此盈抱恨　曠然一夕中

善蘊豈輕售　懷才希國工　誰當念素士　零落歲華空

Written at the end of 775 in Ch'ang-an in response to his friend's "fine words."
Feng is coming from the direction of Loyang through the Hankukuan and Tung-
kuan passes and is coming to take part in the annual civil service examination.
Spring begins on New Year's Day in China. (2/7b)

For Feng Chu

We served apart in separate capitals
I think of you as a tumbleweed too
your arrival brings back the past
for ten years we've held different posts
the year is late and the clouds have settled in
thin homespun is no longer enough
a traveler's lot is a miserable one
you came through the passes in the wind and snow
but a festive wine puts a smile on your face
and your fine words have freshened the air
we began with a belly of regret
and made it last all night
why sell a treasure so cheaply
this cherished talent and rarest of officials
but who pays attention to an honest man
the new year means nothing when you're poor

45

長安遇馮著

客從東方來　衣上灞陵雨　問客何為來　采山因買斧

冥冥花正開　颶颶鸞新乳　昨別今已春　鬢絲生幾縷

Written in the spring of 776 in Ch'ang-an. After arriving in Ch'ang-an, Feng Chu took up residence in the Paling Hills east of the capital, which was an area associated with recluses. Hoping for a government post, he was in the capital to take the official examination and spent the winter and spring preparing. However, Wei's choice of the word *buy* suggests Feng Chu might have also been in the market for an appointment through a back door. He had many friends among other poets living in the capital. Wei's images of spring's annual renewal are meant as encouragements, though we humans have only so many renewals per body. (5/14a)

Meeting Feng Chu in Ch'ang-an

A guest arrives from the east
soaked by Paling rain
I ask what brings him here
a woodsman he says needs to buy an ax
somewhere blossoms are beginning to open
fledgling swallows pirouette overhead
since we last parted it's already spring
how much of your white hair is new

46

送澠池崔主簿

邑帶洛陽道　年年應此行　當時匹馬客　今日縣人迎

暮雨投關郡　春風別帝城　東西殊不遠　朝夕待佳聲

Written in the spring of 776 in Ch'ang-an. Wei's brother-in-law, Ts'ui Cho, is heading east to take up his new position as the third-ranking official in the county seat of Mienchih, which was located on the main road between Ch'ang-an and Loyang. It was 80 kilometers west of Loyang and 300 kilometers east of Ch'ang-an. Nowadays Mienchih is best known for the site that established the Yangshao Neolithic cultural horizon. The route there was through the Tungkuan and Hankukuan passes. (4/8a)

Seeing Off Secretary Ts'ui to Mienchih

Your new post straddles the Loyang Road
you've made this trip every year
but you were a traveler on horseback before
you'll be welcomed by the magistrate now
as you hurry toward the passes in the evening rain
spring wind waves the capital goodbye
it isn't that far between east and west
I'll listen for your voice night and day

47

酒肆行

豪家沽酒長安陌　　一旦起樓高百尺
碧疏玲瓏含春風　　銀題彩幟邀上客
迴瞻丹鳳闕　直視樂遊苑
四方稱賞名已高　　五陵車馬無近遠
晴景悠揚三月天　　桃花飄俎柳垂筵
繁絲急管一時合　　他壚隣肆何寂然
主人無猒且專利　　百斛須臾一壺費
初釀後薄為大偷　　飲者知名不知味
深門潛醞客來稀　　終歲醇醲味不移
長安酒徒空擾擾　　路旁過去那得知

Written in the late spring of 776 in Ch'ang-an. Red Phoenix Gate and the Garden of Delights were both inside the palace. Hence, this allegorical wineshop and its owner must refer to one of the bureaus within the central government and its director. But which or to whom it refers is a mystery. Five Hills was an area thirty or more kilometers northwest of Ch'ang-an centered around the burial mounds of five emperors. It was also the location of some of the wealthiest estates of the T'ang dynasty. (9/2b)

Ballad of the Wineshop

On a Ch'ang-an street where the rich buy their wine
one morning rose a building a hundred feet high
its latticework of jade displayed scenes of spring
its bright signs and banners all welcomed guests
with Red Phoenix Gate behind
and the Garden of Delights in front
all quarters sang its praises and added to its fame
from Five Hills came carriages regardless of the distance
this sunny scene continued through Third Month skies
peach petals decked the tables and willows screened the seats
while an orchestra of strings and flutes played on
other inns and wineshops one by one turned silent
still the owner demanded more profit
the price of a single cup was a hundred sacks of grain
it was strong at first then thin and finally robbery
but patrons knew its name and nothing of its taste
such customers are rare behind one set of doors
where wine is strong all year and its flavor never changes
but the drinkers of Ch'ang-an go merrily stumbling on
along the road they pass it by oblivious to its presence

48

夜偶詩客操公作

塵襟一蕭灑　清夜得禪公　遠自鶴林寺　了知人世空

驚禽翻暗葉　流水注幽叢　多謝非玄度　聊將詩興同

Written in 776 in Ch'ang-an. Master Heng-ts'ao was a monk known to other capital poets, including Wang Wei. In Ch'ang-an, he lived at Chinglung Temple, in the quarter adjacent to where Wei was living. Here, he has just returned from the Yangtze, where he stayed for a time at Holin Temple in the hills south of Chenchiang. The understanding of emptiness, the absence of self-existence, underlies Mahayana Buddhism, of which Zen was one of the most popular schools. Hsuan-tu was the literary name of Hsu Hsun, a recluse of the mid-fourth century who lived near Chenchiang and who excelled at the spontaneous and clear expression of his innermost feelings. He is also credited as being among the first to use Buddhist images and concepts in his poetry. (1/7b)

Composed upon Meeting the Poet, Master Ts'ao, at Night

Once his dusty robe was off
the Zen master appeared this cloudless night
all the way from Holin Temple
though we know the world is empty
birds flutter startled among dark leaves
a stream winds through a secluded garden
my apologies for not being Hsuan-tu
but I still share his joy in verse

49

移疾會詩客元生與釋子法朗
因貽諸曹

對此嘉樹林　獨有戚戚顏　抱瘵知曠職　淹旬非樂閑
釋子來問訊　詩人亦扣關　道同意暫遣　客散疾徐還
園徑自幽靜　玄蟬噪其間　高熄暇遠郊　暮色起秋山
英曹幸休暇　恨恨心所攀

Written in the summer of 776 in Ch'ang-an while Wei was taking a leave of absence from his duties at the Labor Bureau. The identities of Yuan-sheng and Fa-lang are unknown. (1/7a)

Having Requested Time Off Due to Illness, I Meet the Poet Yuan-sheng and the Monk Fa-lang and Accordingly Send This to My Colleagues

Facing this grove of noble trees
I alone looked depressed
missing work due to illness
I knew no pleasure for weeks
until a monk came to inquire
and a poet knocked on my gate
with friends of the Way my cares soon vanished
but my symptoms returned when they left
the garden path now is still and dark
there is only the din of cicadas
from my upper window I can see past the city
evening has reached the autumn hills
my colleagues are happy to be leaving work
but regrets are all I can think of

50

信州錄事參軍常曾
古鼎歌

三年糾一郡　獨飲寒泉井
江南鑄器多鑄銀　罷官無物唯古鼎
彫螭刻篆相錯蟠　地中歲久青苔寒
左對蒼山右流水　云有古來葛仙子
葛仙埋之何不還　耕者鏘然得其間

Written in the summer of 776 in Ch'ang-an. The district of Hsinchou was centered in what is now the town of Shangjao in Kiangsi Province. As its administrative supervisor, Ch'ang Tseng was in charge of correcting abuses and authenticating documents. "Drinking from cold spring wells" refers to his uprightness, and three years was the normal term of office. Ch'ang was later elevated to the position of censor, at which point Wei wrote another poem to him, in 782. Chiangnan (South of the Yangtze) is the term for the area south of the Yangtze's lower reaches. Master Ko was Ko Hsuan, the famous uncle of the equally famous Taoist alchemist Ko Hung. The uncle conducted his experiments with elixirs in the Hsinchou area, and cinnabar was an important ingredient in many such compounds. (10/4a)

Song on the Ancient Tripod of Administrative Supervisor Ch'ang Tseng of Hsinchou

For three years you chastised a whole district
drinking from cold spring wells
the metalwork of Chiangnan is known for its silver
you resigned and came back with only this bronze
carved with dragons and intertwining inscriptions
in the ground so long it's as green as winter moss
on one side a mountain on the other a river
Ko the Immortal long ago they say
Master Ko buried it but never returned
then a farmer plowing struck it with a twang
instead of showing those who don't know its value
why not smelt cinnabar and try to live forever

51

使雲陽寄府曹

夙駕祗府命　冒炎不遑息　百里次雲陽　閭閻問漂溺
上天屢儆氣　胡不均寸澤　仰瞻喬樹顛　見此洪流跡
良苗免湮沒　蔓草生宿昔　頹墉滿故墟　返喜將安宅
周旋涉塗潦　側峭緣溝脈　仁賢憂斯民　賤子甘所役
公堂眾君子　言笑思與覿

Written in the summer of 776 while on a mission to survey flood damage in Yun-yang, a town north of Ch'ang-an on the Ching River. In Wei's capacity in the Labor Bureau, he would have been charged with overseeing rebuilding of roads and bridges — hence the appropriateness of his visit, even if he did volunteer. He must have annoyed those at the prefecture office with his assessment of their concern. But he could afford it. The prefect was Wei's patron, Li Huan. Still, such an attitude betrays the aloofness of an aristocrat who cannot conceal his disdain for bureaucrats who might be better educated but who are not committed to any ideal other than their own welfare. (2/7a)

On a Mission to Yunyang: To the Prefecture Staff

I left at dawn on the prefect's orders
to brave flames and not to dally
a hundred *li* later I reached Yunyang
at every village I asked about flooding
the forces of Heaven keep going astray
why aren't its blessings bestowed more fairly
looking at the tops of tall trees
I could see the traces of disaster
perfectly good crops in the river
creepers growing back already
ancient towns filled with rubble
once-happy homes in ruins
I waded down flooded roads on my tour
whole hillsides were washed away
our wise and kind prefect was concerned for the people
I myself volunteered for this duty
meanwhile you gentlemen at court
gossip and laugh and think about parties

傷
逝

染白一為黑　焚木盡成灰　念我室中人　逝去亦不迴
結髮二十載　賓敬如始來　提攜屬時屯　契闊憂患災
柔素亮為表　禮章夙所該　仕公不及私　百事委令才
一旦入閨門　四屋滿塵埃　斯人既已矣　觸物但傷摧
單居移時節　泣涕撫嬰孩　知妾謂當遣　臨感要難裁
夢想忽如睹　驚起復徘徊　此心良無已　遠屋生蒿萊

Written in the early fall of 776 in Ch'ang-an following the death of his wife. The expression *ssu-jen* (this person) is an old one from the *Book of Songs* and refers to one's wife. (6/8a)

Lamenting My Loss

Like silk that's been dyed
or wood that's now ash
I recall the person I lived with
gone and not coming back
to whom I was wedded for twenty years
who respected me as if we just met
our betrothal occurred during troubled times
our separations were due to disasters
a model of gentleness and simplicity
she was courteous and always proper
but public office has no room for oneself
and my duties undercut her beauty
this morning when I entered the women's quarters
the rooms were covered with dust
ever since this person left
whatever I touch is painful
a widower now I pass the time
wiping our children's tears
I try to push my fantasies away
but these feelings are hard to stop
suddenly my daydreams look real
startled I begin pacing again
this heart is utterly relentless
and our house is surrounded by weeds

53

往富平傷懷

晨起凌嚴霜　慟哭臨素帷
駕言百里塗　惻愴復何為
昨者仕公府　屬城常載馳
出門無所憂　返室亦熙熙
今者掩筠扉　但聞童稚悲
丈夫須出入　顧爾內無依
衝恨已酸骨　何況苦寒時
單車路蕭條　迴首長逶遲
飄風忽截野　嘹唳鴈起飛
昔時同往路　獨往今詎知

Written in the late fall of 776 in Ch'ang-an following the death of Wei's wife. He was serving as administrator in the Labor Bureau and was often sent to towns within its jurisdiction—towns such as Fuping, fifty kilometers northwest of Ch'ang-an. On the way there, he would have had to pass through Kaoling, where he served earlier as magistrate. The "white shroud" refers to the funerary covering but also to the frost. (6/8a)

Grieving on the Way to Fuping

A bitter frost fell this morning
before the white shroud I cried
ordered on a hundred-*li* journey
what good would sorrow do
earlier in the prefecture office
I ran errands to towns in the district
leaving home without any worries
always coming back happy
now when I close my rickety gate
I hear our children crying
but a father has to go forth
even when there's no mother at home
swallowing remorse hurts me inside
all the more in this bitter cold
in a one-person cart on a road so bleak
I look back and keep slowing down
a rising wind lashes the plain
geese cry out and fly off
in the past we traveled this road together
I never thought I'd be on it alone

54

出還

昔出喜還家　今還獨傷意　入室掩無光　銜哀寫虛位

悽悽動幽幔　寂寂驚寒吹　幼女復何知　時來庭下戲

咨嗟日復老　錯莫身如寄　家人勸我飧　對桉空垂淚

Written in the late fall of 776 in Ch'ang-an after Wei's short assignment to Fuping. Wei Ying-wu and his wife had one son and two daughters. The women's quarters would have had their own separate, albeit small, courtyard. The epitaph Wei wrote for his wife is at the back of this book. (6/8a)

Returning Home after a Trip

In the past I was glad to come home
but to sadness I now return
entering our closed sunless room
I stifle my grief and write the epitaph
I lift the dark curtain in pain
startled by a cold desolate breeze
our younger daughter doesn't realize
she still comes into the courtyard to play
I sigh every day feeling older
dazed by the transience of life
my relatives urge me to eat
at the table my tears fall in vain

55

送終

日月獲其良　蕭蕭車馬悲　祖載發中堂
生平同此居　一旦異存亡　終復委山岡
奄忽踰時節　斯須亦何益　歲月始難忘
行出國南門　南望鬱蒼蒼　日入乃云造
晨遷俯玄廬　臨訣但遑遑　方當永潛翳
俯仰遽終畢　封樹已荒涼　獨留不得還
童稚知所失　啼號捉我裳　即事猶蒼卒
仰視白日光　欲去結中腸
慟哭宿風霜

Written in the late fall of 776. Wei buried his wife on the Tuling Plateau south of
Ch'ang-an in the Wei clan burial plot, the exact location of which is still unknown.
Wei's son was less than a year old and his older daughter was already in her early
teens, but his younger daughter was only five. (6/8b)

The Funeral

Suddenly the time is here
the auspicious chosen date
the team of horses whinny
the hearse departs the ancestral hall
this was where we lived our lives
until we were parted by death
what good is this brief moment
if we just end up in the hills
the cortege left by the city's South Gate
southward I gazed toward the ragged ridges
the sun went down and clouds appeared
I cried all night in the bitter wind
into the tomb I looked at dawn
saying farewell I could only tremble
into the ground the coffin vanished
I looked up at the sun's bright light
a moment later it was over
even the graveside trees looked bleak
I stood unable to move
I couldn't leave with my heart in a knot
our daughter sensed what we had lost
she wailed and clutched my robe
this is still too sudden
the months and years too hard to forget

56

任鄠令渼陂遊眺

野水灧長塘　煙光亂晴日　氛氳綠樹多　蒼翠千山出
遊魚時可見　新荷尚未密　屢往心獨閑　恨無理人術

Written in the early summer of 777 in Huhsien. Wei's patron, Li Huan, arranged for his appointment to this town fifty kilometers southwest of Ch'ang-an. It provided Wei with a place at which to grieve the loss of his wife, but it also advanced him a notch on the appointment ladder, as Huhsien was a more important county than Kaoling. The Mei River flows out of the Chungnan Mountains and joins the Laoyu river southwest of this county seat better known today for the primitive paintings of its farmers. In Wei's day, the river was used to form a reservoir three kilometers west of town. (7/7b)

Letting My Eyes Roam at Mei Reservoir While Serving as
Magistrate of Huhsien

White water surges along the embankment
mist swirls in a sunny sky
green is taking over the trees
there's jade on a thousand mountains
fish are swimming up to the surface
lotuses aren't thick yet
I come here to be alone with my thoughts
I regret lacking social skills

57

子規啼

高林滴露夏夜清　南山子規啼一聲

鄰家嬌婦抱兒泣　我獨展轉何時明

Written in the summer of 777 in Huhsien, nearly a year after the death of his wife. The cuckoo is normally a harbinger of spring, but its plaintive cry is also associated with loss, perhaps because it's usually heard in the middle of the night when heartbroken people can't sleep. (8/12a)

The Call of the Cuckoo

Dew drips from tall trees on a clear summer night
in the hills to the south a cuckoo calls
the widow next door comforts her child
I turn in bed and wait for first light

58

過昭國里故第

不復見故人　一來過故宅　物變知景暄　心傷覺時寂
池荒野筍合　庭綠幽草積　風散花意謝　鳥還山光夕
宿昔方同賞　詎知今念昔　緘室在東廂　遺器不忍覷
柔翰全分意　芳巾尚染澤　殘工委筐篋　餘素經刀尺
收此還我家　將還復愁惕　永絕攜手歡　空存舊行迹
冥冥獨無語　杳杳將何適　唯思今古同　時緩傷與戚

Written in the fall of 777 on a visit to Ch'ang-an. The main north-south road in Ch'ang-an was Red Bird Street, which began at the Forbidden City's Red Bird Gate. Two blocks south of Red Bird Gate and three blocks west were Kuangte Quarter and the prefecture office where Wei once worked in the Labor Bureau. Six blocks south of Red Bird Gate and three blocks east was Chaokuo Quarter, where he lived with his wife and which he revisits here. It was considered an out-of-the-way residential area. (6/9b)

Passing Our Old Place in Chaokuo Quarter

Passing our old home
I don't see anyone I know
things have changed and the air feels warm
my heart suffers from the loneliness of the season
the pond is choked with wild bamboo
the courtyard is overgrown with unfamiliar plants
the wind scatters fading flowers
birds return to darkening hills
in the past we enjoyed this together
how strange to be recalling those times
her room in the eastern wing is closed
I can't bear to look at the things she left
her calligraphy brush and writing kit
her perfumed scarf still damp
tools she left in her chest
pieces of silk she cut with her knife
I collected these things to bring back
but bringing them back would just cause more grief
parted forever from the joys we shared
why keep the traces she left behind
words can't express something so dark
and to that distant place I can't go
but the past and present I think are one
and time soothes heartache and sorrow

59

昭國里第聽元老師

彈琴

竹林高宇霜露清　朱絲玉徽多故情
暗識啼烏與別鶴　秖緣中有斷腸聲

Written in the fall of 777, most likely during the same visit (see previous poem) to his old home in Ch'ang-an. The *ch'in/qin*, or Chinese zither, is played across the knees or on a small table (which helps amplify the sound), one hand plucking its silk (now steel) strings and the other hand adjusting the length of the vibrating strings by pressing down. In choosing where to press, the player selects a point along a series of inlaid jade or mother-of-pearl circles, which indicates the harmonic, and of which there are thirteen. "Calling Crows" and "Departing Cranes" are the names of two tunes for the zither. Master Yuan Ch'ang was a teacher, apparently of music. Wei addresses another poem to him in which Yuan plays the transverse flute. (8/7b)

Listening to Master Yuan Play the Ch'in in Chaokuo Quarter

On bamboo leaves and rooftops the autumn dew is clear
vermilion strings and jade harmonics multiply old feelings
Calling Crows and Departing Cranes are tunes I somehow recognize
containing as they do the sounds of a breaking heart

60

答東林道士

紫閣西邊第幾峯　茅齋夜雪虎行蹤
遙看黛色知何處　欲出山門尋暮鍾

Written in the winter of 777 while serving as magistrate of Huhsien County. Tzuke (Purple Pavilion) was the name of a peak in the Chungnan Mountains fifteen kilometers southeast of town. *Tung-lin* means "eastern grove." Judging from Wei's reply, this Taoist priest's poem must have mentioned finding tiger tracks outside his hut in the snow. The South China tiger is now nearly extinct, but it once ranged over all of China. It is bigger than a German shepherd but only about half the size of a Siberian tiger. Some zoologists consider it the ancestor of all tigers. (5/7a)

In Reply to Taoist Master Tung-lin

How many peaks are you west of Tzuke
in your thatched hut on a snowy night beside those tiger tracks
if I knew where you were in that distant blackness
I would follow your evening bell all the way up the mountain

61

再遊西郊渡

水曲一追遊　遊人重懷戀　嬋娟昨夜月　還向波中見
驚禽棲不定　流芳寒未徧　攜手更何時　佇看花似霰

Written in the spring of 778 while serving as magistrate of Huhsien. This was one of eight poems Wei wrote about his visits to this area along the Feng River halfway between Huhsien and Ch'ang-an. Apparently someone planted some plum trees along the river. (7/7b)

Visiting the Ferry in the Western Suburbs Again

Where the river winds I reflect on my travels
a traveler lost in reminiscence again
the moon last night was so lovely
I've come back to see it in the waves
birds won't roost where they feel afraid
or a fragrance spread where it's cold
when will I hold someone's hand again
the flowers overhead look like sleet

62

紫閣東林居士叔緘賜松英丸

捧對忻喜蓋非塵侶之所當服

輒獻詩代啟

碧澗蒼松五粒稀　侵雲采去露沾衣　夜啟羣仙合靈藥　朝思俗侶寄將歸

道場齋戒今初服　人事葷羶已覺非　一望嵐峯拜還使　腰間銅印與心違

Written in the spring of 778 while serving as magistrate of Huhsien. Wei's Taoist friend, who is living near Tzukefeng, or Purple Pavilion Peak, sends Wei some pills compounded of pine pollen and other herbal ingredients. The five-needle pine native to the Chungnan Mountains is known as the Huashan pine. An official carried his seal of office at the waist, held there by a ribbon. (2/9a)

Shu-chien, Layman Tung-lin of Tzuke, Sends Me Pine
Pollen Balls, Which I Am Glad to Receive—Though They
Are Not Meant to Be Eaten by People in the World of Dust.
I Respond with a Poem Instead of a Letter

From five-needle pines in beryl blue gorges
gathered in the clouds along with the dew
you made your magic pills after summoning immortals
and thinking of benighted friends sent some down to me
fasting at an altar today I finally ate them
suddenly the stench of mundane life seems wrong
gazing at your cloud-wrapped peak I send this back in thanks
the brass seal at my waist pulls against my heart

63

扈亭西陂燕賞

景景朝陽時　悠悠清陂望　嘉樹始氳氤　春遊方浩蕩
況逢文翰侶　愛此孤舟漾　綠野際遙波　橫雲分疊嶂
公堂日為倦　幽襟自茲曠　有酒今滿盈　願君盡弘量

Written in the spring of 779 while Wei served as magistrate of Huhsien County. Huting was an old name for the area northwest of the county seat. This was once the state of Hu during the Hsia dynasty 4,000 years ago. West Reservoir was fed by the Mei River and was also known as Mei Reservoir. In addition to supplying the town with drinking water, it was a popular place for recreation. Tu Fu also wrote a poem about boating there. (1/7b)

Picnicking at West Reservoir in Huting

In the radiant morning sunshine
I survey the boundless clear lake
the tall trees are beginning to leaf out
spring outings starting to become grand
especially upon meeting friends of the brush
who love to float around in a boat
where the green countryside and far waves meet
and bands of clouds divide layered ridges
when days at court leave officials weary
their unspoken feelings here find release
with wine today in good supply
I trust we'll exceed every measure

64

休沐東還貴里示端

宦遊三十載　田野久已疎　休沐遂茲日　一來還故墟
山明宿雨霽　風暖百卉舒　泓泓野泉潔　熠熠林光初
竹木稍摧翳　園場亦荒蕪　俯驚鬢已衰　周覽昔所娛
存沒惻私懷　遷變傷里閭　欲言少留心　中復畏簡書
世道良自退　榮名亦空虛　與子終攜手　歲晏當來居

Written in the summer of 779 while serving as magistrate of Huhsien. Wei began serving away from home in 751 when he joined the imperial guard in Ch'ang-an. Hence, it wasn't quite thirty years that he had been away. His family home was in Choukuei Village on the Tuling Plateau southeast of Ch'ang-an near what is now Weichu Village. During the T'ang it was located in Wannien County, Hungku Township. His cousin, Wei Tuan, was living there between appointments. It was Wei's day off, which he refers to euphemistically as "bathing day." The mountains to the south are the Chungnan Mountains. (2/8b)

Returning East to Choukuei Village on Bathing Day: For Tuan

For thirty years an itinerant official
I no longer recognized the fields
but since it was my day to bathe
I traveled back to our village
the rains had stopped and the mountains were clear
the wind was warm and plants were thriving
the mountain-fed streams were deep and pure
the forests beginning to dance with light
but the bamboo was looking a bit sad
and the garden was nothing but weeds
and I was startled by the gray at your temples
and the sight of where we once played
and the heartbreaking news of departures
and the changes that had ravaged this place
I wanted to speak but who would care
and now I'm worrying about reports again
I'd be better off giving up this worldly career
fortune and fame are so hollow
compared to finally being with you
here in my declining and future years

65

東郊

吏舍跼終年　出郊曠清曙　楊柳散和風　青山澹吾慮
依叢適自憩　緣澗還復去　微雨靄芳原　春鳩鳴何處
樂幽心屢止　遵事跡猶遽　終罷斯結廬　慕陶真可庶

Written in the summer of 779 in Huhsien. The countryside east of Huhsien and
west of Ch'ang-an became Wei's favorite place to ramble. This was, in fact, the
area where he would actually follow the example of his hero, T'ao Yuan-ming
(365–427)—and much sooner than he thought. T'ao was a poet who extolled
country living and who became a model for all those who aspired to nonurban
alternatives. After serving in government for a few years, T'ao simply quit one day
and retired to a village at the foot of Lushan. (7/10b)

East of Town

Stuck in an office all year
I left the city for the wide-open dawn
where willow catkins soothed the wind
and blue mountains stilled my cares
where everything green put me at ease
where I followed a stream and followed it back
where a light rain covered a flowering plain
and spring doves were calling unseen
I keep suppressing my love of seclusion
I'm invariably busy at work
but someday I'll retire and build a hut here
to be like Old T'ao would be sweet

66

澧上西齋寄諸友

絕岸臨西野　曠然塵事遙　清川下邐迤　茅棟上岧嶤
酌月愛佳夕　望山屬清朝　俯砌視歸翼　開衿納遠飆
等陶辭小秩　効朱方負樵　閑遊忽無累　心跡隨景超
明世重才彥　雨露降丹霄　羣公正雲集　獨予忻寂寥

Written in the early fall of 779 at Shanfu Temple. The Feng River flows out of the Chungnan Mountains and passes through the eastern part of Huhsien County on its way to join the Wei River west of Ch'ang-an. In the sixth month, Wei Ying-wu's friend and patron, Li Huan, was banished to Tuanchou, and Wei was demoted from magistrate of Huhsien to magistrate of Leyang, a small town east of Ch'ang-an. Rather than take up a post he considered beneath him, Wei resigned, citing illness, and took up residence southeast of Huhsien. The place he chose was Shanfu Temple, fifteen kilometers southwest of Ch'ang-an on the

My Western Study on the Feng River: To My Friends

The steep bank overlooks the countryside to the west
the world of dust is far far away
a clear river winds below me
a thatched roof towers above
I enjoy the moonlight and especially fine evenings
and I gaze at mountains until dawn
I look at stone steps and at birds coming home
and I open my robe to every faint breeze
like Old T'ao who resigned a minor post
or Master Chu who hauled firewood
suddenly I wander without burdens
my thoughts float along detached
our enlightened age values skill and refinement
and dew is falling from Cinnabar Heaven
the just are gathering like clouds
I alone prefer solitude

east shore of the Feng River just north of where it is joined by the Chueh River.
Ever the aristocrat, Wei insists on calling his humble residence a *chai* (study).
T'ao Ch'ien (T'ao Yuan-ming) was the model of all officials wishing they had the
guts to quit and live the simple life. Likewise, Chu Mai-ch'en of the Han dynasty
preferred to spend his days reading and supported himself by selling firewood.
Cinnabar Heaven refers to the palace, where steps leading to the throne were
painted red. (2/9a)

67

答崔主簿倬

朗月分林靄　遙管動離聲　故驪良已阻　空宇澹無情
窈窕雲鴈沒　蒼茫河漢橫　蘭章不可答　沖襟徒自盈

Written in the early fall of 779 after Wei declined to accept his new post as magistrate of Leyang, retiring instead to a Buddhist temple between Huhsien and Ch'ang-an. Secretary Ts'ui Cho was married to one of Wei's cousins. He was known for his interest in Taoist alchemy and lived to be over ninety. At the time of this poem, Ts'ui was serving as secretary to the magistrate of Mienchih County, just west of Loyang. The poem to which Wei replies appears to have raised the subject of his wife's death. (5/7a)

In Reply to Secretary Ts'ui Cho

The bright moon divides the mist from the forest
far off a flute plays a song of parting
cut off now from former joys
I don't feel a thing in this empty place
wild geese disappear into distant clouds
the river of stars spans a dark void
I can't reply to your elegant verse
to pour out my heart would be useless

68

寺居獨夜寄崔主簿

幽人寂不寐　木葉紛紛落　寒雨暗深更　流螢度高閣

坐使青燈曉　還傷夏衣薄　寧知歲方晏　離居更蕭索

Written in the fall of 779 while living in retirement at Shanfu Temple. Wei was especially close to Ts'ui Cho and wrote more poems to him than to anyone else. Wei's reference in the first line to a *yu-jen* (recluse) is to himself. When Buddhism first arrived in China, monasteries were built around a stupa of solid bricks and earth that contained the remains of an eminent monk. Later on, some temples erected pagodas instead, with interior stairs up to the top where people could look out. I've met a lot of hermits in China who tell me, "That new guy on the mountain won't last one winter." Delighting in solitude isn't enough. Even solitude gets lonely. (2/10a)

Alone at Night at My Monastic Residence: To Secretary Ts'ui

The recluse is in bed but not asleep
leaves are falling in flurries
a cold rain makes the late night darker
fireflies are gone from the tower
the blue flames of dawn are no help
I still suffer from a thin summer robe
I didn't realize the year was so late
or living apart was so lonely

69

閑居贈友

補吏多下遷　罷歸聊自度
閑居養痾瘵　守素甘葵藿
青苔已生路　綠筠始分籜
草玄良見誚　杜門無請託

園盧既蕪沒　煙景空澹泊
顏鬢日衰耗　冠帶亦寥落
夕氣下遙陰　微風動疎薄
非君好事者　誰來顧寂寞

Written in the early summer of 780. Substitute officials were appointed to vacant, low-level posts without needing to go through the formalities required of higher posts. Although Wei did enter officialdom without taking the usual exams, he is being a bit hard on himself here. Still, he was "demoted" for his association with Li Huan, who was banished then executed. Unwilling to take up his new, less-prestigious, post, he returned to the area where he had been serving and took up residence at a hermitage near the Chungnan Mountains. Country temples often included a few huts within or adjacent to their walls, as well as the standard shrine hall or two. In the background here is Yang Hsiung (53 B.C.–A.D. 18), a Han-dynasty poet and philosopher, whose writings, especially his *Taihsuan-ching* ("Treatise on the Great Mystery"), were criticized by his superficial counterparts at court. (2/9b)

Living in Retirement: For a Friend

A substitute official repeatedly demoted
I quit and retired to reflect
my hut and garden are overgrown with weeds
it's a misty deserted tranquil place
living in retirement I nurse my ills
I keep life simple and enjoy wild plants
my hairline is steadily receding
and my formal wear looks sad
a layer of moss covers the road
the new bamboos have begun sprouting leaves
in the haze of dusk the far crescent sets
a light breeze awakens distant thoughts
but writing about Mystery would only earn me scorn
and my closed gate greets no callers
if not for a well-wisher like you
who would look in on the lonely

70

澧上寄幼遐

寂寞到城闕　惆悵返柴荊　端居無所為　念子遠徂征
夏晝人已息　我懷獨未寧　忽從東齋起　兀兀尋澗行
冒暑叢榛密　披翫孤花明　曠然西南望　一極山水情
周覽同遊處　逾恨阻音形　壯圖非旦夕　君子勤令名
勿復久留燕　蹉跎在北京

Written in the summer of 780 while living in retirement at Shanfu Temple. Yu-hsia was the personal name of Li Tan, with whom Wei conducted a lifelong exchange of poems. Wei went to Ch'ang-an to see his friend, only to discover he had been sent to the northern garrison city of Taiyuan, which was once the capital of the ancient state of Yen. Back at his retreat along the Feng River, he recalls their time together. In another poem, Wei refers to his own residence at or near the temple as the Western Study. Either he moved to the other side of the temple, or he's simply marking his point of departure. Or perhaps *tun* (east) is a mistake for *hsi* (west). The Feng River was, after all, west of the temple. (2/10b)

On the Feng River: To Yu-hsia

Feeling lonely I traveled to the city gates
sadly I'm back at my old door
living in peace with nothing to do
I think of you on a distant journey
summer days when people are resting
I'm here alone with unsettled thoughts
suddenly I'm leaving the Eastern Study
unconsciously following a stream
caught in a thicket of brambles
stopping to examine a lone flower's beauty
gazing into the boundless southwest
at nothing but mountains and rivers
I look around where we once walked
cut off alas from your face and voice
the plans of youth need more than a day
a gentleman has to work for his name
don't stay too long in the land of Yen
languishing away in that northern city

71

效陶彭澤

霜露悴百草　時菊獨妍華　物性有如此　寒暑其奈何
掇英泛濁醪　日入會田家　盡醉茅簷下　一生豈在多

Written in the fall of 780 at Shanfu Temple. T'ao P'eng-ts'e is another name for T'ao Yuan-ming, Wei's hero, who once served as magistrate of Pengtse County but found official life tedious and retired to a hut in a farming village. Wei is celebrating the ninth day of the ninth month, when men congratulate one another on their continued virility and drink wine infused with chrysanthemum petals. (1/6a)

In Imitation of T'ao P'eng-ts'e

When other plants bow to the frost
chrysanthemums alone show their beauty
this is the nature of things
there's no changing the seasons
I sprinkle their petals in homemade wine
at sunset I sit down with farmers
under thatched eaves all of us drunk
life is about more than plenty

72

寓居灃上精舍寄於張二舍人

萬木藂雲出香閣　西連碧潤竹林園
高齋猶宿遠山曙　微霰下庭寒雀喧
道心淡泊對流水　生事蕭疎空掩門
時憶故交那得見　曉排閶闔奉明恩

Written in the winter of 780 at Shanfu Temple. The two men to whom Wei addresses this poem, Yu Shao and Chang Chi, worked in the Secretariat, where their jobs included composing drafts of imperial edicts. The "stream" is the Feng River. The light in the last line also refers to imperial favor. (2/11a)

Living at My Hermitage on the Feng: To Imperial Secretaries Yu and Chang

From a sea of trees and clouds rise incense-perfumed halls
to the west is a stream of jade and a garden of bamboo
there's me in my lofty study and distant dawn-lit peaks
a fine sleet in the courtyard and chattering winter birds
I face the flowing water and cultivate tranquil thoughts
but to life's affairs and loneliness I close my door in vain
sometimes I recall old friends and wonder where they are
I open the gate at dawn and greet the welcome light

73

答崔都水

深夜竹庭雪　孤燈案上書

不遇無為化　誰復得閑居

Written in the winter of 780 at Shanfu Temple. Ts'ui Cho was married to one of Wei Ying-wu's cousins and had been called back to the capital from his post in Mienchih and promoted to serve as one of the two commissioners in charge of the Directorate of Waterways. Ts'ui was a Taoist practitioner, and the cultivation of inaction is praised in the *Taoteching*. But here it is also a critical reference to Emperor Hsuan-tsung, who was given to conceiving of himself and his reign in Taoist terms. As Lao-tzu says in his *Taoteching*: 2, "The sage performs effortless deeds and teaches wordless lessons." It was the emperor's inattention to government affairs that was blamed for the An Lu-shan Rebellion. Wei was a member of the palace guard when the rebellion began. (5/9a)

In Reply to Commissioner Ts'ui

A courtyard of bamboo and late-night snow
a lone lantern a book on the table
if I hadn't encountered the teaching of no effort
how else could I have gained this life of leisure

74

答暢校書當

偶然弃官去　投跡在田中　日出照茅屋　園林養愚蒙
雖云無一資　罇酌會不空　且忻百穀成　仰歎造化功
出入與民伍　作事靡不同　時伐南澗竹　夜還澧水東
貧塞自成退　豈為高人蹤　覽君金玉篇　彩色發我容
日日欲為報　方春已徂冬

Written in the winter of 780 at Shanfu Temple. The friend to whom Wei took so long to reply was working in the central government's Construction Commission at the time. He was also a well-known poet, and both men exchanged a number of poems. For the name in the title, I've replaced the character *yang* with the nearly identical *ch'ang*, which occurs in later editions. The stream to the south was the Chueh River. (5/8b)

In Reply to Gentleman-in-Attendance Ch'ang Tang

I just happened to quit my post
and end up in the countryside
where the rising sun lights thatched huts
and gardens and groves support simple folk
though I'd agree I'm without means
my wine cup is rarely empty
I delight in ripening grain
and sigh at the work of creation
in step with villagers dawn to dusk
there's nothing they do I don't
I cut bamboo along the stream to the south
and return at night to the Feng's east shore
I retired because of incompetence
it wasn't to follow a higher path
I read your essay of jade and gold
its beautiful hues lit up my face
day after day I've wanted to reply
that was in spring and now it's winter

75

観田家

微雨眾卉新 一雷驚蟄始 田家幾日閑 耕種從此起
丁壯俱在野 場圃亦就理 歸來景常晏 飲犢西澗水
飢劬不自苦 膏澤且為喜 倉廩無宿儲 徭役猶未已
方慚不耕者 祿食出閭里

Written in the spring of 781 at Shanfu Temple. The fifteen-day solar period known as Insects Astir begins March fifth or sixth when the first thunder of the year traditionally stirs hibernating creatures, large and small. The date was used in almanacs to signal the beginning of work in the fields and occurred a month or so after the Lunar New Year holidays. After harvesting their vegetables and melons in the fall, farmers turned their plots into threshing floors by beating the earth until it was hard. Hence, the vegetable plots needed to be reclaimed every spring. West Creek probably refers to the Feng River, which was just west of the temple. Farm families were also required to send one adult male to take part in public works projects. Officials were paid in grain and silk, which they then exchanged for cash and other goods. (7/8a)

Watching Farmers

The rain is light and plants are new
one clap of thunder and insects are stirring
farmers have but a few days of rest
before plowing and planting begin
everyone able is off in the fields
or putting gardens in order
the light is fading when they come home
from taking their calves to West Creek to drink
hunger and exhaustion don't get them down
happiness is moist fertile soil
nothing is left in their bins from last year
and still there's compulsory service
those who don't farm should be embarrassed
their salaries come from a village

76

種瓜

率性方鹵莽　理生尤自疎　今年學種瓜　園圃多荒蕪
眾草同雨露　新苗獨翳如　直以春揺迫　過時不得鋤
田家笑枉費　日夕轉空虛　信非吾儕事　且讀古人書

Written in the spring of 781 at Shanfu Temple on the Feng River. In this poem, Wei recalls the story of an official who lost his position at the end of the Ch'in dynasty (221–207 B.C.) and supported himself by growing melons outside the city wall. Despite his change in fortune, the official was not only content with his new lot, he prospered, and the fame of his melons spread throughout the land. (8/10a)

Planting Melons

When I follow my nature I'm rash
too careless to earn a living
this year I tried planting melons
in a garden that was mostly weeds
the plants all shared the rain and dew
but mine ended up in the shade
and once spring work got busy
the time for hoeing was past
the farmers laughed at my useless efforts
from dawn to dusk resulting in nothing
clearly this isn't my kind of work
I'll stick with ancient texts instead

77

幽居

貴賤雖異等　出門皆有營　獨無外物牽　遂此幽居情
微雨夜來過　不知春草生　青山忽已曙　鳥雀繞舍鳴
時與道人偶　或隨樵者行　自當安蹇劣　誰謂薄世榮

Written in the spring of 781 at Shanfu Temple. The birds are looking for a place to nest, perhaps under Wei's eaves where it's nice and quiet. It's hard to say if Wei's use of *chien* (lame) here is figurative or refers to his chronic foot ailment. From the Taoist point of view, only the person who is truly content is worthy of veneration. (8/5b)

Living in Seclusion

The rich and the poor are different
but they all go forth to earn a living
only someone without material attachments
can pursue this life of seclusion
after the lightest of rains last night
spring plants all at once appeared
dark mountains were suddenly bright
birds circled my hut and sang
sometimes I join men of the Way
sometimes I follow woodcutters
I accept being lame and incompetent
but who says I disdain worldly glory

78

園林晏起寄昭應韓明府盧主簿

田家已耕作　井屋起晨煙　園林鳴好鳥　閑居猶獨眠
不覺朝已晏　起來望青天　四體一舒散　情性亦忻然
還復茅簷下　對酒思數賢　束帶理官府　簡牘盈目前
當念中林賞　覽物遍山川　上非遇明世　庶以道自全

Written in the spring of 781. Wei Ying-wu and Han Chih were previously colleagues in Ch'ang-an when Wei worked in the Labor Bureau and Han in the Revenue Bureau. At the time of this poem, Han was serving as magistrate of Chaoying County (Lintung), just east of Ch'ang-an. Secretary Lu was possibly Lu Keng, whom Wei had known in Loyang. The smoke is from burning the detritus of last year's harvest. The last couplet has been echoed by Chinese intellectuals ever since there were intellectuals and goes back to "The Fisherman's Song," attributed to Ch'u Yuan (d. 278 B.C.), which urges service when service does some good and otherwise retirement in the countryside. (3/4a)

Waking Late in My Garden: To Magistrate Han and Secretary Lu in Chaoying

Farmers have already started to plow
thick smoke is rising from their yards
birds are singing sweetly from garden trees
being retired I was still asleep
unaware the day was so late
I got up and gazed at the azure sky
I stretched my limbs
and felt happy indeed
then I went back below thatched eaves
poured some wine and considered fine men
adjusting their belts on their way to the office
with nothing but documents to fill their days
wishing they were here in the woods
enjoying the sight of mountains and streams
unless you're living in enlightened times
why not work on yourselves instead

79

始除尚書郎別善福精舍

簡略非世器　委身同草木　逍遙精舍居　飲酒自為足
累日曾一櫛　對書常懶讀　社臘會高年　山川恣遊矚
明世方選士　中朝懸美祿　除書忽到門　冠帶便拘束
愧忝郎署跡　謬蒙君子錄　俯仰垂華纓　飄颻翔輕轂
行將親愛別　戀此西澗曲　遠峯明夕川　夏雨生眾綠
迅風飄野路　迴首不遑宿　明晨下煙閣　白雲在幽谷

Written in the early summer of 781 upon leaving Shanfu Temple. The original poem also included this note: "On the nineteenth day of the fourth month I went from being magistrate of Leyang to vice director of the Bureau of Review in the Department of State Affairs." When Wei was appointed magistrate of Leyang in the summer of 779, instead of refusing the post, he asked for a leave of absence, which became tantamount to resignation after one hundred days. Normally, wine is forbidden in Buddhist temples. But Wei's status, even though he had fallen on hard times, would have permitted him some latitude in such matters. An official's hat included strings with tassels that were tied under the chin. "White clouds" refer to those who live without restrictions. (4/9b)

On Being Appointed to the Department of State Affairs and Leaving Shanfu Hermitage

Too careless to work in public office
I cast my lot with the weeds and trees
living in a hermitage however I pleased
having wine I felt was enough
I combed my hair every few days
and rarely looked at a book
on festival days I met local elders
and let my eyes wander among mountains and streams
but times are brighter and I've been selected
the court has announced my name
the letter of appointment is at the gate
my hat and my belt are tied
ashamed to be filling a vice director's post
I've unjustly accepted a gentleman's title
my hat tassels dangle as I bob along
in a carriage that floats on the wind
I'm leaving close friends behind
and this bend of West Creek I love
the far peaks shine in the water at sunset
summer rains have turned everything green
a sudden gust blows across the dirt road
I turn to look but can't stay another night
tomorrow I'll be below perfumed towers
and white clouds will be in dark valleys

80

答趙氏生伉

暫與雲林別　忽陪鴛鷺翔　看山不得去　知爾獨相望

Written in the summer of 781 in Ch'ang-an shortly after Wei left his hermitage on the Feng River and accepted an appointment in the Department of State Affairs. Presumably Chao was at the family estate south of Ch'ang-an. High officials were often likened to mandarin ducks, as they wore the most ornate of robes and attended court in pairs. (5/9a)

In Reply to My Nephew Chao K'ang

I recently left the woods and clouds
suddenly I'm in step with mandarins
I see the mountains but I can't leave
and I know you're there waiting for me

81

答端

郊園夏雨歇　閑院綠陰生
物色坐如見　離抱悵多盈

職事方無効　幽賞獨違情
況感夕涼氣　聞此亂蟬鳴

Written in the late summer of 781 in Ch'ang-an while serving at the Bureau of Review. It didn't take Wei long to regret leaving his thatched hut. I'm not sure where Wei's cousin, Wei Tuan, was living at the time. But given the sentiments in the sixth line, it would seem that Tuan wasn't in Ch'ang-an. T'ang historical sources note two residences for Wei Tuan inside Ch'ang-an: the first in the Chingjen Quarter southeast of Red Bird Gate, the second in the Hsinchang Quarter, a bit farther to the southeast. But he also served outside Ch'ang-an. The same sources say that Wei Tuan (737–819) died in office at the age of eighty-three. The Sian area still gets most of its rain in the summer. (5/9a)

In Reply to Tuan

In suburban gardens summer rains have stopped
green shade spreads across vacant yards
working in an office doesn't do any good
and goes against my love of seclusion
suddenly I see your image before me
and the sadness of separation fills my heart
especially when I feel the cool evening air
and hear the din of cicadas

82

夜直省中

河漢有秋意　南宮生早涼　玉漏殊杳杳　雲闕更蒼蒼

華燈發新燄　輕煙浮夕香　顧跡知為忝　束帶愧周行

Written in the seventh month of 781 in Ch'ang-an while serving at the Department of State Affairs. The River of Stars is the Milky Way, and South Palace was where Wei worked. All junior officials were required to take turns doing night duty there, where time was kept with a waterclock, and where the first light of dawn was announced from an adjacent tower. The last line's *chou-hang* means "the trade of Chou," which refers to the advent of a bureaucratic class in the first millennium B.C., during the Chou dynasty. (8/5a)

Night Duty at the Department of State

The River of Stars is pointing toward fall
South Palace is getting cold early
the jade waterclock is too dim to see
the cloud tower is even darker
the flowered lanterns are finally lit
the fragrance of the night floats in
considering my embarrassing past
I'm ashamed to be following a civil servant's path

83

憶灃上幽居

一來當復去　猶此厭樊籠　況我林栖子　朝服坐南宮
唯獨問啼鳥　還如灃水東

Written in 782 in Ch'ang-an. Wei's post in the Department of State Affairs was located in South Palace. The hermitage where he was living prior to returning to the capital was on the east shore of the Feng River, about forty kilometers southeast of Ch'ang-an. (6/5b)

Recalling My Secluded Residence on the Feng

Jumping one way then back again
they still hate their cages
how much more this woodland creature
inside South Palace in court attire
who has to ask other birds
how things are on the Feng's east shore

84

話舊

存亡三十載　事過悉成空　不惜霑衣淚　併話一宵中

Written in 782 in Ch'ang-an. Wei added a note to this poem: "Written in tears after talking in the garden with my older brother and sister about former events in the Lanling, Chunghsien, and Huaichen quarters." The quarters to which he refers were those in which their father and grandfather lived in Ch'ang-an. Thirty years earlier, Wei was serving in the palace guard. But in and around 752, Ch'ang-an witnessed dozens of executions and forced suicides, if not coerced retirements, in the struggle for power at court between the factions of Li Lin-fu, Wang Hung, and Yang Kuo-chung. Members of the Wei clan would have found it hard avoiding being swept up in these events that precipitated the An Lu-shan Rebellion. This is one of the few places where Wei mentions his older brother and sister. This is also one of the few poems in which Wei suggests the decline of his family's fortunes was not gradual. (6/11b)

Talking about the Past

They left this world thirty years ago
we lost everything after that
I couldn't keep tears from soaking my robe
we didn't stop talking all night

Chuchou

(782–785) / 58 poems

同德精舍舊居傷懷

洛京十載別　東林訪舊扉　山河不可望　存歿意多違
時遷跡尚在　同去獨來歸　還見窗中鴿　日暮遠庭飛

Written in the summer of 782 when Wei passed through Loyang on the way to his new assignment as magistrate of Chuchou. When Wei resigned his post as deputy magistrate of Loyang County in 766, he and his family lived off and on at Tungte Monastery in the suburbs southeast of the city until he finally returned to Ch'ang-an in the spring of 774. This is one of the last times Wei refers to his wife in a poem. East Grove was the name of a forested parkland southeast of Loyang between the Lo and Yi rivers. It was common for worshipers to buy caged birds and release them at temples to gain merit. (6/10b)

Heartbreak at Our Old Dwelling at Tungte Hermitage

Ten years after leaving Loyang
I visited our East Grove doorway
I couldn't look at the landscape
confronted by thoughts about life and death
time has moved on but her traces remain
we left here together but I'm back alone
I can still see pigeons through the window
circling the courtyard at sunset

86

逢楊開府

少事武皇帝　無賴恃恩私　身作里中橫　家藏亡命兒
朝持樗蒲局　暮竊東鄰姬　司隸不敢捕　立在白玉墀
驪山風雪夜　長楊羽獵時　一字都不識　飲酒肆頑癡
武皇升仙去　憔悴被人欺　讀書事已晚　把筆學題詩
兩府始收跡　南宮謬見推　非才果不容　出守撫煢嫠
忽逢楊開府　論舊涕俱垂　坐客何由識　唯有故人知

Written in the summer of 782 on the way to take up his new post in Chuchou. Wei and Yang both served together in the palace guard in the early 750s, but Yang has since advanced to the position of area commander, tantamount to a regional warlord, while Wei is traveling to a more modest post. "Emperor Wu" is a reference to Emperor Hsuan-tsung, who was sometimes called Emperor Shen-wu. He died in 762. Lishan was the location of the hot springs northeast of Ch'ang-an where emperors spent the coldest part of each winter. During the Ch'in dynasty, Willow Palace was built northwest of Ch'ang-an across the Wei River. Here it

Meeting Commander Yang

In our youth we served Emperor Wu
and shamelessly presumed on his favor
we acted like local bullies
spoiled brats and lawless jerks
during the day we played games of dice
at night we abducted neighborhood girls
the commandant didn't dare touch us
we stood on alabaster steps
and those snowswept nights on Lishan
and archery hunts at Willow Palace
we couldn't read a word
we drank ourselves silly instead
then our lord joined the immortals
while we suffered disgrace
it was too late for us to study
or to learn how to improvise poems
two prefects finally took me in
then by mistake I was called to South Palace
but lacking talent I could only fail
and was sent to care for widows and orphans
suddenly now I meet Commander Yang
and we talk about the past until we cry
how do you recognize an exile
only an old friend would know

is merely a location near which royal hunts were conducted. The two prefects
under whom Wei served without having to pass the civil service exam were those
in charge of Loyang and Ch'ang-an counties. South Palace was another name for
the Department of State Affairs in which Wei worked for one year before being
sent to Chuchou. A magistrate's responsibilities were often referred to euphe-
mistically as "caring for widows and orphans." Obviously, Wei considers his new
assignment a form of banishment. (5/14b)

87

大梁亭會李四栖梧作

梁王昔愛才　千古化不泯　至今蓬池上　遠集八方賓
車馬平明合　城郭滿埃塵　逢君一相許　豈要平生親
入仕三十載　如何獨未伸　英聲久籍籍　臺閣多故人
置酒發清彈　相與樂佳辰　孤亭得長望　白日下廣津
富貴良可取　揭來西入秦　秋風旦夕起　安得客梁陳

Written in the late summer of 782 in Kaifeng on the way to Chuchou. Kaifeng was the capital of the ancient state of Liang. During the second century B.C., the king was known for attracting the literati of his day, and he entertained his guests at a number of water-based venues, one such being Pengchih Lake, forty-five kilometers southwest of Kaifeng. While visiting the lake, Wei met the man to whom he addresses this poem. It turns out they have friends in common, as well as off-and-on government service stretching back over thirty years. Wei's new friend has received an appointment back in Ch'ang-an (the land of Ch'in) and will be leaving the land of Liang and Ch'en (the small state where the lake was located), while Wei will be continuing on via the Kaifeng and Grand canals—there is no longer anyone like King Liang to detain him. (1/6a)

Meeting Li Hsi-wu at Taliang Pavilion

The talented men cherished by King Liang
haven't been forgotten by the ages
here at Pengchih Lake today
visitors come from every direction
their carts and horses arrive with the dawn
covering city walls with dust
though we met but a moment ago
who needs a lifetime to become friends
you've been an official for thirty years
and not the only unfulfilled one
your illustrious name has long been mentioned
in the Great Hall we have many friends
so let's have some wine and play our zithers
and enjoy an auspicious day together
from this lone pavilion we can watch
the sun disappear at the ford
wealth and honor are yours for the taking
as you head west into Ch'in
autumn wind blows from dawn to dusk
and guests can't stay in Liang or Ch'en

88

夕次盱眙縣

落帆逗淮鎮　停舫臨孤驛

浩浩風起波　冥冥日沉夕

人歸山郭暗　鴈下蘆洲白

獨夜憶秦關　聽鍾未眠客

Written in the early fall of 782 on the way to Chuchou. Hsuyi was a small town on the southern shore of the ever-flooding Huai River. Wei arrived here at sunset after traveling down the Kaifeng Canal. A nationwide network of post stations was used by the central government for its couriers and emissaries on official business. Wei identifies with the geese. He, too, is heading south. Ch'in Pass was another name for the Hanku Pass between Ch'ang-an and Loyang. It was where Lao-tzu reportedly wrote his *Taoteching*. But here it's a reference to the land west

Stopping for the Night in Hsuyi County

Lowering our sail at a Huai River town
we tied up beside a lone post station
as the wind whipped the waves higher
and the sun's setting light grew dimmer
people returned to darkened village walls
wild geese landed on white island sands
alone at night recalling Ch'in Pass
a sleepless traveler listens to the bell

of the pass that once belonged to the ancient state of Ch'in and where Wei's home was located. During the T'ang dynasty, Buddhist temples rang what they called the Bell of Impermanence at midnight. This poem is reminiscent of Chang Chi's more famous poem, written about the same time, while he anchored near Suchou. "Crows caw the moon sets frost fills the sky / river maples fishing fires care-plagued sleep / coming from Cold Mountain Temple outside the Suchou wall / the sound of the midnight bell reaches a traveler's boat. (6/7a)

89

淮上喜會梁川故人

江漢曾為客　相逢每醉還　浮雲一別後　流水十年間

歡笑情如舊　蕭疎鬢已斑　何因不歸去　淮上對秋山

Written in the early fall of 782 on the way to Chuchou. The location of Liang-chuan is uncertain. Some editions have Liangchou, which was the name for Hanchung, on the other side of the Chungnan Mountains south of Ch'ang-an. The two men apparently met more than ten years earlier on Wei's trip down the Grand Canal to Yangchou in the fall of 769. Still far from home, they meet once more in fall, this time in the city of Huaiyin (Huai-an). Chianghan (and its reverse: Hanchiang) was one of several names used to refer to the administrative area centered in Yangchou that included the southern half of the Huai River watershed. (1/6b)

Happily Meeting an Old Friend from Liangchuan on the Huai

When we were both guests in Chianghan
whenever we met we left drunk
we've been drifting clouds ever since
following rivers ten years now
the happiness we feel is the same
though our hair has thinned and turned gray
why haven't we gone home
and left these autumn hills on the Huai

90

淮上即事寄廣陵親故

前舟已眇眇　欲渡誰相待　秋山起暮鍾　楚雨連滄海
風波離思滿　宿昔容鬢改　獨鳥下東南　廣陵何處在

Written in the early fall of 782 on the way to Chuchou. Stopping where the Huai
River intersects the Grand Canal at Huaiyin — about 100 kilometers short of the
Yellow Sea — Wei hears the bell of a Buddhist temple on a nearby hill and recalls
someone he met during his earlier visit to Kuangling (Yangchou) in the fall/win-
ter of 769. This region was once part of the ancient state of Ch'u. While waiting
for the next boat, and it's possible he had other business in Huaiyin, Wei sends
his thoughts to his friend by means of a passing wild goose, the mail carriers of
the hopelessly separated. From Huaiyin, it was another 150 kilometers south-
east to Yangchou. (2/6a)

Events on the Huai: To a Dear Friend in Kuangling

The earlier boat is already faint
I was hoping to cross but it wouldn't wait
from autumn hills comes the evening bell
it's raining in Ch'u all the way to the sea
the windblown waves recall our parting
the way I once looked has changed
a lone bird heading southeast
asks the way to Kuangling

91

揚州偶會前洛陽盧耿主簿

楚塞故人稀　相逢本不期　猶存袖裏字　忽怪鬢中絲

客舍盈樽酒　江行滿篋詩　更能連騎出　還似洛橋時

Written in the early fall of 782 in Yangchou. Yangchou was once part of the ancient state of Ch'u. As late as the T'ang dynasty, the Yangtze was still considered the frontier—although a frontier whose revenues were absolutely essential to the survival of the central government. Both Wei and Lu served together in Loyang. Both men had to cross Loyang Bridge every day on their way to and from the morning audience at the headquarters of Honan Prefecture. But the bridge and the area around it was also a place where people engaged in various forms of recreation. Wei was on his way to Chuchou to take up his post as magistrate and was reporting to Yangchou, which was the administrative center for the region of which Chuchou was a part. (1/6b)

In Yangchou Unexpectedly Meeting Former Secretary Lu Keng of Loyang

In the land of Ch'u friends are rare
meeting you here was unexpected
I've kept your letters close to my heart
how strange to see white in your hair
our cups overflow with an innkeeper's wine
our luggage is full of river-travel poems
may we ride forth together again
as we once did on Loyang Bridge

92

贈崔員外

一別十年事　相逢淮海濱　還思洛陽日　更話府中人
且對清觴滿　寧知白髮新　忽忽何處去　車馬冒風塵

Written in the fall of 782 on the way to Chuchou. The identity of the man to whom Wei writes this poem is unknown. Apparently, it wasn't his brother-in-law, Ts'ui Cho, who was back in Ch'ang-an. His title indicates he was an auxiliary appointee to an unspecified post. The two men clearly met each other earlier while Wei was still in Loyang serving as administrator of the Garrison Command of Honan Prefecture (770–773). Huaihai refers to the Huai River watershed in general and in particular to the area where the Grand Canal intersects with the Yangtze. (3/7a)

To Supernumerary Ts'ui

Ten years after we parted
we meet on the shores of Huaihai
recalling our days in Loyang
we discuss prefecture colleagues
and facing cups of fine wine
wish our white hair was new
where are you hurrying off to
braving the dust and wind of the road

93

白沙亭逢吳叟歌

龍池宮裏上皇時　羅衫寶帶香風吹
滿朝豪士今已盡　欲話舊遊人不知
白沙亭上逢吳叟　愛客脫衣且沽酒
問之執戟亦先朝　零落艱難卻負樵
親觀文物蒙雨露　見我昔年侍丹霄
冬狩春祠無一事　歡遊洽宴多頒賜
嘗陪夕月竹宮齋　每返溫泉灞陵醉
星歲再周十二辰　爾來不語今為君
盛時忽去良可惜　一生坎壈何足云

Written in the fall of 782 in Yangchou, on the way to Chuchou. White Sand Pavil-
ion was south of Yangchou near the north shore of the Yangtze. Dragon Pool
was a large spring-fed pond adjacent to Hsingching Palace in the eastern part
of Ch'ang-an and was the scene of banquets and imperial parties. The star that
makes its circuit around the zodiac every twelve years is Jupiter. Twenty-four
years earlier would have been in 758. Since Wei's service in the imperial guard
ended in 756, he is roughing out the years here, as he does elsewhere. Paling is
the name of an imperial grave mound dating back to the Han dynasty, but the
name also refers to the area along the Pa River east of Ch'ang-an where people
saw off friends. The hot springs were at the foot of Lishan, a bit farther to the
northeast. (10/2a)

Song on Meeting Old Wu at White Sand Pavilion

In Dragon Pool Palace when our lord was alive
the jeweled belts and brocade robes and the perfumed wind
but all the court officials of those days are gone
no one would understand if I told them what we did
then I meet Old Wu at White Sand Pavilion
and he pawns his robe to buy a guest wine
I ask him about the halberdiers of that earlier reign
they're hauling firewood now in these troubled times
enjoying imperial favor we watched everything
those years in attendance on cinnabar-colored clouds
the winter hunt and spring sacrifice nothing escaped us
the outings and the feasts and all that we received
taking part on moonlit nights in Bamboo Palace fasts
coming back drunk from Paling or the hot springs
the twelve-year star has gone around us twice
I haven't shared these thoughts until today with you
the sudden end of that great age fills me with regrets
what is there to say about a life of failure

94

秋夜一絕

高閣漸凝露　涼葉稍飄閨　憶在南宮直　夜長鍾漏稀

Written in the fall of 782 after Wei arrived in Chuchou. In the first line, the term
kao-ke (high-structure) referred to any multistoried building. In this case, the
magistrate's second-floor residence is probably meant. The Department of State
Affairs was located in Ch'ang-an's South Palace, where Wei served off and on
from 774 to 782. Junior staff members were required to take turns staying over-
night, just in case an urgent memorial needed drafting prior to the dawn audi-
ence. Time in the palace at night was kept with a waterclock, the dripping sound
of which contrasts here with the gathering dew and falling leaves of Wei's new
post in the provinces. (8/8b)

Quatrain on an Autumn Night

The upper story is seeing more dew
brittle leaves are falling lightly against my door
I think back to serving at night in South Palace
hour after hour the clock dripping slower

95

新秋夜寄諸弟

兩地俱秋夕　相望共星河　高梧一葉下　空齋歸思多
方用憂人瘼　況自抱微痾　無將別來近　顏鬢已蹉跎

Written in the fall of 782 in Chuchou. This poem would have been written on the Mid-Autumn Festival, the full moon of the eighth month, when families and friends gather outside and watch the moon together. The River of Stars is the Milky Way. The paulownia has huge leaves, and once the first leaf drops, the rest aren't far behind. (3/4a)

New Fall Night: To My Cousins

Our two worlds share this autumn night
we see the same River of Stars
a leaf drops from a towering paulownia
thoughts of going home fill my empty rooms
I worry about the hardships of the people
then too I have my own minor ills
I won't be leaving anytime soon
but my hairline has already slipped away

96

答王郎中

臥閣枉芳藻　覽旨悵秋晨　守郡猶覊寓　無以慰嘉賓
野曠歸雲盡　天清曉露新　池荷涼已至　窗梧落漸頻
風物殊京國　邑里但荒榛　賦繁屬軍興　政拙媿斯人
髦士久臺閣　中路一漂淪　歸當列盛朝　豈念臥淮濱

Written in the fall of 782 in Chuchou. Wei was sent to serve out someone else's term as magistrate. Therefore, his post did not include a full salary. The references to dew, lotuses, and falling paulownia leaves indicate midautumn. Wei met Wang while both men were serving in the Department of State Affairs (the Great Hall). Wang is now between assignments and traveling. Wei only mentions Wang's surname, but the two were friends and exchanged half a dozen poems. The prefecture of Chuchou was in the Huainan (South Huai) District, whose administrative center was in Yangchou. Hence, Wei is stuck in Huainan and only figuratively on the Huai. (5/9b)

In Reply to Director Wang

Your fine lines are wasted on me in my office
I read them with regret this autumn dawn
I may be magistrate but I'm still a lodger
with nothing to welcome an honored guest
the countryside is free of yesterday's clouds
the sky is clear and the morning dew is fresh
the lotuses in the pond have felt the chill
the paulownia outside is letting go its leaves
the capital is known for stylish scenes
this town is all brambles and weeds
and more and more taxes to raise more armies
such imbecilic policies make me feel ashamed
your eminence served in the Great Hall many years
now in midcareer you've been set adrift
but you'll be returning to that illustrious court
and why think of someone stuck here on the Huai

97

送中弟

秋風入疎戶　離人起晨朝　山郡多風雨　西樓更蕭條
嗟予淮海老　送子關河遙　同來不同去　沉憂寧復消

Written in the late fall of 782 in Chuchou. Chuchou was bordered on two of its four sides by the slopes of Huangfushan and Langyashan, and there were plenty of other mountains in the prefecture of which Wei was magistrate. But calling Chuchou a *shan-chun* (mountain town) also reflects Wei's assessment of his post as far too provincial for his liking. After less than a month or so in Chuchou, Wei is already identifying himself with this region—stuck as he is in the southern edge of the Huai River watershed. The road back to the capital began at the city's West Gate and led northwest and eventually through the Hankukuan and Tung-kuan passes on the Yellow River. The man to whom Wei addresses this poem accompanied him from Ch'ang-an and is now returning. The expression *older brother* was figurative, and some editions title this poem "Seeing off Ts'ui Hsiao-yi." (4/11a)

Seeing Off My Older Brother

Autumn cold slips through a poorly made door
a traveler is up at dawn
this mountain town is all wind and rain
West Gate Tower more desolate still
Old Huaihai can only sigh
seeing you off for distant passes
we came here together but you're leaving alone
if only these cares would leave too

98

郡齋感秋寄諸弟

首夏辭舊國　窮秋臥滁城　方如昨日別　忽覺徂歲驚
高閣收煙霧　池水晚澄清　戶牖已淒爽　晨夜感深情
昔遊郎署間　是月天氣晴　授衣還西郊　曉露田中行
采菊投酒中　昆弟自同傾　簪組聊挂壁　焉知有世榮
一旦居遠郡　山川間音形　大道庶無累　及茲念已盈

Written on the ninth day of the ninth month of 782 in Chuchou and addressed to his four cousins back at the family homestead south of Ch'ang-an. Wei celebrated this day at home with his cousins the previous fall, when he was still serving in the Department of State Affairs. It was a custom to have new clothes made in the ninth lunar month in preparation for winter. On the ninth day of that month men celebrated their longevity (actual or hoped-for) with wine infused with chrysanthemum petals. Hanging one's hat and sash on the wall suggests a temporary reprieve from office. (3/4b)

In My Prefecture Quarters Affected by Autumn: To My Cousins

I left the capital at the start of summer
I was sleeping in Chuchou by the end of fall
it's as if we parted yesterday
I'm suddenly startled by the passage of time
even when the upper story is free of fog
the pond doesn't clear until dusk
outside my windows looks bleak
night and day my heart feels heavy
last year visiting the Department of State
the weather this month was sunny
in the western suburbs collecting my clothes
I walked through dew-covered fields
I picked chrysanthemums to put in the wine
and drank it all down with my cousins
I hung my hat and sash on the wall
what did I care about worldly fame
now I'm living in a distant town
with mountains and rivers keeping us apart
the Tao doesn't come with many burdens
until memories pile up on this day

99

冬至夜寄京師諸弟兼懷崔都水

理郡無異政　所憂在素飡　徒令去京國　羈旅當歲寒
子月生一氣　陽景極南端　已懷時節感　更抱別離酸
私燕席云罷　還齋夜方闌　遼幕沉空宇　孤燭照床單
應同茲夕念　寧忘故歲歡　川塗恍悠邈　涕下一闌干

Written in the winter of 782 in Chuchou. Wei Ying-wu's cousins and his brother-in-law, Ts'ui Cho, are all back in Ch'ang-an. Wei arrived in Chuchou in fall, but in winter he is already visiting towns under his jurisdiction. The winter solstice is celebrated as the rebirth of *yang* energy and is a time when family members usually return home to be together. Both the land and water routes through the Huai watershed were periodically under the control of the Li Hsi-lieh, who had revolted and set up an independent kingdom during this period. Hence, transportation back to Ch'ang-an was uncertain. (3/5a)

Winter Solstice Night: To My Cousins in the Capital and Thinking of Director Ts'ui

Governing a prefecture takes no special skill
what bothers me is eating for free
leaving the capital was senseless
I'm still on the road in midwinter
but a breath is born in this darkest month
when the sun is at its southern limit
I suffer the seasonal malaise
not to mention the pain of separation
at a private banquet I called it quits
returning to my quarters just before dawn
distant scenes merged with the empty sky
a lone candle lit my blanket
I keep thinking we should be together this night
then I try to forget last year's joys
the water route home is long and uncertain
and my bed frame is wet with tears

100

元日寄諸弟兼呈崔都水

一從守茲郡　兩鬢生素髮　新正加我年　故歲去超忽
淮濱益時候　了似仲秋月　川谷風景溫　城池草木發
高齋屬多暇　怊悵臨芳物　日月昧還期　念君何時歇

Written on New Year's Day of 783 in Chuchou. The Chinese add a year to their ages at New Year. The *fang-wu* (fragrant stuff) refers to rice wine. Li Hsi-lieh was occupying the territory between the Yangtze and Loyang. However, communication by government courier was still carried on by back roads and circuitous routes. (3/5a)

New Year's Day: To My Cousins and to Pass On to Commissioner Ts'ui

Since I took over this district
my temples have begun to turn white
the new year has added to my age
and the old year is a long way away
there's an extra season here on the Huai
it seems like the middle of autumn
the air in the valleys is warmer
and plants along the moat are sprouting
but there's nothing to do in my fancy quarters
even this fragrant stuff is depressing
the date I'll return is a mystery
or when I'll stop thinking of you

101

郡樓春燕

眾樂雜軍鞞　高樓邀上客　思逐花光亂　賞餘山景夕
為郡訪彫瘵　守程難損益　聊假一杯歡　暫忘終日迫

Written on New Year's Day of 783 in Chuchou. The Chinese consider New Year's Day the beginning of spring. Here, Wei entertains the officials under his command. (1/8a)

Spring Banquet in the Magistrate's Hall

The orchestra includes a cavalry drum
the great hall welcomes distinguished guests
we recall the madness of our quest for beauty
enjoying the traces of a mountain dusk
we ran around this district until we were exhausted
keeping order regardless if it helped or hurt
let us now lift our cups with joy
and forget for a night our daily troubles

102

春遊南亭

川明氣已變　巖寒雲尚擁　南亭草心綠　春塘泉脈動
景煦聽禽響　雨餘看柳重　逍遙池館華　益媿專城寵

Written in the early spring of 783 in Chuchou. Nanting, or South Pavilion, was located in the city's South Park, where the signs of spring always show up first. Wei's sense of responsibility for the hardships of the people under his care overwhelms even the pleasures of an early spring outing. (7/9a)

Visiting Nanting Pavilion in Spring

The valleys are brighter and the air feels different
but winter clouds still mask the cliffs
the plants at Nanting show signs of green
and the spring is rippling across the pond
with warmer weather I hear more birds
and willows look thicker from all the rain
lounging at a waterside inn is lovely
but adds to the spoiled magistrate's shame

103

賦得暮雨送李冑

楚江微雨裏　建業暮鍾時　漠漠帆來重　冥冥鳥去遲

海門深不見　浦樹遠含滋　相送情無限　沾襟比散絲

Written in the early spring of 783 on the Yangtze across from Chienyeh, or Nan-
ching. Li Wei was a fellow official. Wei Ying-wu was serving in Chuchou but is see-
ing his friend off on the Yangtze, which was also called the River of Ch'u because
this region once belonged to the ancient state of Ch'u. The river's entrance into
the East China Sea was still several hundred kilometers farther east, but Ocean
Gate was also the name of a mountain not far downstream from Nanching near
the city of Chenchiang. (4/6b)

On Encountering Evening Rain While Seeing Off Li Wei

River of Ch'u in light rain
evening bells of Chienyeh
rows of sails spreading out
birds disappearing slowly
Ocean Gate too far to see
riverside trees a distant green
there's no end to goodbye
a pair of silk streams soak my sleeves

104

社日寄崔都水及諸弟羣屬

山郡多暇日　社時放吏歸　坐閣獨成悶　行塘閱清輝

春風動高柳　芳園掩夕扉　遙思里中會　心緒悵微微

Written in the spring of 783 in Chuchou. Earth God Day falls forty-five days after New Year's, or midway through the second lunar month. Wei's brother-in-law, Ts'ui Cho, was serving as water commissioner in Ch'ang-an. Chuchou was bordered by mountains on the south and the west, but to call it a "mountain town" was also meant to suggest its remoteness from the capital and Wei's home. (3/5b)

Earth God Day: To Water Commissioner Ts'ui and My Cousins and Relatives

Festivals abound in this mountain town
on Earth God Day officials stay home
sitting upstairs feeling bored
I walked out to the pond for the light
spring wind rustled the willows
I shut the garden gate at dusk
as I thought of you together in our village
disappointment slipped into my heart

105

寄職方劉郎中

相聞二十載　不得展平生　一夕南宮遇　聊用寫中情
端服光朝次　羣列慕英聲　歸來坐粉闈　揮筆乃縱橫
始陪文翰遊　歡燕難久并　予因謬忝出　君為沉疾嬰
別離寒暑過　荏苒春草生　故園茲日隔　新禽池上鳴
郡中永無事　歸思徒自盈

Written in the spring of 783 in Chuchou. The Bureau of Operations was in charge of military maps, frontier fortifications, and signal systems. Its director was a man named Liu Wan, whom Wei must have heard about in 763, when he was deputy magistrate of Loyang, and whom he must have met in the spring of 782, when he was serving in the Department of State Affairs (South Palace), where he wrote reports and assessments. Liu has remained in Ch'ang-an, where he suffers from an unspecified illness or perhaps from the court's displeasure. (3/5b)

To Director Liu at the Bureau of Operations

I heard your name for twenty years
but I couldn't imagine your life
until we met at South Palace one night
and briefly expressed our feelings
your perfect attire lit up our ranks
the officials at court extolled your fame
I went back to whitewashed halls
and employed my brush on assessments
at first I joined the literary outings
but I didn't last at the banquets
then I was wrongly sent off
while you were beset by illness
a summer and winter have passed since we parted
spring plants are flourishing again
my old garden is far away
and new birds are singing by the moat
there's never any work in this prefecture
but thoughts of going home fill my mind in vain

106

贈李儋侍御

風光山郡少　來看廣陵春　殘花猶待客　莫問意中人

Written in the late spring of 783 in Chuchou. Bored in Chuchou, Wei visits Yangchou (Kuangling), which was the administrative headquarters for the Huainan District, of which Chuchou was a part. The "fading flowers" indicate late spring, but they also suggest a visit to a big-city brothel. (3/6a)

For Attendant Li Tan

There's not much excitement in a mountain town
I went to see spring in Kuangling
the fading flowers still welcomed my visit
and no one asked if there was someone in my heart

107

訓柳郎中春日歸揚州南郭見別之作

廣陵三月花正開　花裏逢君醉一迴　南北相過殊不遠　暮潮從去早潮來

Written in the late spring or early summer of 783 following a visit to Yangchou. It is the last stretch of the Changchiang, or Long River, from Yangchou to the Yellow Sea, which locals call the Yangtze. Even though the city is 200 kilometers upstream, the daily tide differential is as much as two meters. (5/4b)

*Written in Response to Court Gentleman Liu on Meeting
and Parting at the South Wall on the Way Back to Yangchou
on a Spring Day*

The third month in Yangchou the city was in bloom
we met and got drunk among the flowers
we were going different directions but not very far
what the evening tide took away the morning tide brought back

108

寒食日寄諸弟

禁火曖佳辰　念離獨傷抱
見此野田花　心思杜陵道
聯騎定何時　予今顏已老

Written in the late spring of 783 in Chuchou. Cold Food occurred 150 days after the Winter Solstice, or just before Grave Sweeping Day, and included a ban on the use of fire to heat or cook for up to three days. Wei was with his cousins at their home on the Tuling Plateau during this time the previous year. (3/5b)

Cold Food Day: To My Cousins

The fire ban darkens an auspicious day
I still feel the pain of our parting
seeing these flower-covered fields
reminds me of the trails on Tuling
when will we ride together again
I'm feeling much older today

109

三月三日寄諸弟兼懷崔都水

暮節看已謝　茲晨愈可惜　風澹意傷春　池寒花斂夕
對酒始依依　懷人還的的　誰當曲水行　相思尋舊跡

Written in late spring of 783 in Chuchou. The "winding river" refers to the Chu-chiang Waterway southeast of Ch'ang-an and just north of Wei's family home on the Tuling Plateau. (3/6a)

The Third Day of the Third Month: To My Cousins and Thinking of Commissioner Ts'ui

The season seems to be ending early
this morning felt sadder still
the wind stirs a heartbreaking spring
and the pond chills a flowerless night
the longer I look at the wine
the clearer you become
who is that walking along the winding river
looking for my footprints and thinking of me

110

滁州西澗

獨憐幽草澗邊生　上有黃鸝深樹鳴
春潮帶雨晚來急　野渡無人舟自橫

Written in the spring of 783 in Chuchou. After spending the day wandering through the countryside west of Chuchou, Wei returned so late he had to pull himself across on the cable boat kept there for that purpose. Commentators are divided over whether this is a simple descriptive poem or whether political implications lie beneath its surface, in which case the neglected plants would refer to virtuous, but unappreciated, officials and the orioles to those whose voices are heard but ignored. The last couplet recalls similar lines in the *Book of Odes* which refer to spurned genius and also suggest that political conditions are worsening and there is nothing left to do but to save oneself. Then again, maybe this is just a poem about having the countryside to oneself on a day in spring. (8/11a)

Chuchou's West Stream

I love unnoticed plants that grow beside a stream
orioles singing overhead somewhere in the trees
at dusk the current quickens fed by springtime rains
I pull myself across on an unmanned country ferry

III

遊瑯琊山寺

受命恤人隱　茲遊久未遑　鳴騶響幽澗　前旌耀崇岡
青冥臺砌寒　綠縟草木香　填壑躋花界　疊石構雲房
經製隨巖轉　繚繞豈定方　新泉泄陰壁　高蘿蔭綠塘
攀林一栖止　飲水得清涼　物累誠可遣　疲痾終未忘
還歸坐郡閣　但見山蒼蒼

Written in the late spring of 783 in Chuchou. Langya Temple was built on Langyashan only a decade or so before Wei Ying-wu arrived. It would have been impressive, as it was built along a series of cliffs halfway up the mountain with funds supplied by Emperor Tai-tsung. The temple was also where the poet-monk Stonehouse (Ch'ing-hung Shih-wu) lived for a number of years in the early fourteenth century. As magistrate, Wei was accompanied by attendants who carried red banners and cleared the path before him. The mountain was only five kilometers south of Chuchou and would have been easily visible from Wei's residence in town (the magistrate's quarters). It was also a favorite destination of Ou-yang Hsiu when he served as magistrate of Chuchou two centuries later. He built his Drunkard's Pavilion, which still stands, alongside the wide, cold stone trail that runs through the canyon. (7/12a)

Visiting Langyashan Temple

I was ordered to relieve people's suffering
I didn't have time for such an outing before
the calls of my escort echo through the canyon
their banners illuminate the ridge
the sky-dark stone steps feel cold
the new green foliage smells sweet
gullies were filled in to create this realm of bliss
and rocks piled up to make rooms in the clouds
built to conform with the cliffs
they wind along with no set direction
fresh springs drip down sunless walls
overhead vines shade emerald ponds
I climbed through the trees to a place I could rest
where I tasted water that was pure and cool
material burdens I know can be abandoned
but I can't forget the overworked masses
back in the magistrate's quarters
all I see is a mountain of green

112

南塘泛舟會元六昆季

端居倦時燠　輕舟泛迴塘　微風飄襟散　橫吹繞林長
雲澹水容夕　雨微荷氣涼　一寫惆勤意　寧用訴華觴

Written in the summer of 783 in Chuchou. The summer heat in the Yangtze watershed can be debilitating. Wei and his friend are boating with some sing-song girls and drifting along the southern part of the moat that encircled the city wall. The image of a robe's lapels being ruffled is a standard reference to exposing one's innermost feelings; the flute is a harbinger of thoughts of home; and the lotus is a symbol of transcendence, as it blooms above the water, while rooted in the mud below. Yuan Liu (son number-six) was another name for Yuan K'uang, whose father, Yuan Yi, was serving at court. The phrase *k'un-chi* (elder brother) is euphemistic here. (1/8b)

Boating on South Lake with Elder Brother Yuan Liu

Taking time off in the enervating heat
we drifted in a skiff along the city moat
a light wind blew open our robes
a flute echoed through the woods
thin clouds darkened the water
a fine rain cooled the lotus-scented air
rather than pour out our cares
we raised our cups to the flowers

113

寄楊協律

吏散門閣掩　鳥鳴山郡中　遠念長江別　俯覺座隅空

舟泊南池雨　簟卷北樓風　併罷芳樽燕　為愴昨時同

Written in the late summer of 783 in Chuchou. I'm wondering if the remnants of a typhoon aren't passing through the neighborhood: no one at work, the birds all chattering in confused anticipation, anything that might blow away tied down. Although Chuchou is a few hundred kilometers inland, it still sees a typhoon or two toward the end of every summer. Yang Ling is meant here. The two men exchanged several poems, and it was to Yang Ling that Wei married his older daughter. (3/6a)

To Secretary Yang

Colleagues have scattered and gates are closed
the calling of birds fills a mountain town
our parting on the Yangtze seems so long ago
I notice the empty mat beside me
the boats on South Lake are moored because of rain
the screens at North Tower are rolled up due to wind
wine-tasting parties are canceled
I regret our time together has passed

114

效園聞蟬寄諸弟

去歲郊園別　聞蟬在蘭省　今歲臥南譙　蟬鳴歸路永

夕響依山郭　餘悲散秋景　緘書報此時　此心方耿耿

Written in the early fall of 783 in Chuchou. Orchid Hall was another name for the Department of State Affairs where Wei was serving until he was appointed magistrate of Chuchou in the summer of 782. Hence the garden to which he is refering must be close by—perhaps the royal garden outside the northeast wall of Taming Palace in Ch'ang-an. Just beyond it was the Pa River Bridge where travelers said goodbye. Nanchiao was another name for Chuchou. (3/4b)

In a Suburban Garden Hearing Cicadas: To My Cousins

Parting last year in a suburban garden
we heard cicadas in Orchid Hall
this year I'm ensconced in Nanchiao
where cicadas sing the road home is long
the sounds of dusk echo along the outer wall
my lingering sadness fades in the autumn light
sealing this letter I send this report
of a heart that burns too bright

115

郡中對雨贈元錫兼簡楊凌

宿雨冒空山　空城響秋葉　沉沉暮色至　淒淒涼氣入
蕭條林表散　的皪荷上集　夜霧著衣重　新苔侵履濕
遇茲端憂日　賴與嘉賓接

Written in the early fall of 783 in Chuchou. Both Yuan Hsi and Yang Ling were close friends. Both visited Wei the year after his arrival in Chuchou. The three men exchanged a number of poems. (3/5a)

Rainy Day at the Prefecture Office: For Yuan Hsi and a Note to Yang Ling

Yesterday's rain still shrouds deserted hills
autumn leaves echo through an empty town
the somber colors of evening are here
and the chill air of fall has arrived
the trees look barren and bleak
lotus pads shimmer with raindrops
night fog weighs down my clothes
fresh moss soaks through my shoes
this was such a dismal day
thankfully I spent it with guests

答楊奉禮

多病守山郡　自得接嘉賓
臨觴獨無味　對榻已生塵
煙波見棲旅　景物具昭陳
白事廷吏簡　閑居文墨親
應當整孤棹　歸來展殷勤

不見三四日　曠若十餘旬
一詠舟中作　洒雪忽驚新
秋塘唯落葉　野寺不逢人
高天池閣靜　寒菊霜露頻

Written in the fall of 783 in Chuchou. The vice director of ceremonials was in charge of court rituals and also guided visitors in proper decorum. Rather than rowing a boat with two oars, the Chinese have traditionally used a single oar, or scull, at the stern. (5/10b)

In Reply to Vice Director for Ceremonials Yang

With so many ills and a provincial assignment
I'm glad to receive honored guests
if no one visits for three or four days
it seems like months on end
wine has no taste when I drink alone
I notice the dust on the adjacent couch
but once I'm in a boat singing
and a sprinkling of snow turns everything new
the mist and waves beg for an outing
the scenery is all on display
autumn ponds dotted with leaves
country temples where no one else goes
filling out records is a waste
writing when I'm free is better
the sky is clear and the lake pavilion peaceful
chrysanthemums are blooming in the cold
you should get out that oar
come back and show me your feelings

117

送楊氏女

永日方感感
爾輩況無恃
對此結中腸
賴茲託令門
孝恭遵婦道
居閑始自遣

出門復悠悠
撫念益慈柔
義往難復留
仁恤庶無尤
容止順其猷
臨感忽難收

女子今有行
幼為長所育
自小闕內訓
貧儉誠所尚
別離在今晨
歸來視幼女

大江泝輕舟
兩別泣不休
事姑貽我憂
資從豈待周
見爾當何秋
零淚緣纓流

Written in the fall of 783 in Chuchou. Wei addresses this poem to his older daughter. The man she is marrying is Yang Hsieh-lu, or Yang Ling, with whom Wei exchanged several poems. The reference to the lack of someone to lean on, etc., is to her mother, who died seven years earlier, when she would have been around ten. The river up which she is traveling to her new home is the Yangtze. (4/11a)

Seeing Off My Daughter to the Yangs

Such a long day is too painful
your departure even more upsetting
my daughter you're about to travel
up the Great River in the flimsiest of boats
you didn't have anyone to lean on
nor their compassion or comfort
you yourself raised your sister
now neither of you can stop crying
this ties my heart in knots
but I can't keep you from your rightful journey
from childhood you lacked guidance at home
I worry about you with your in-laws
as I send you off to that good family
kindness and sympathy are rarely scolded
humility and frugality in fact are esteemed
provisions and attendants won't be lacking
piety and respect is the wifely path
in all that you do follow their counsel
after you leave this place today
how many falls before I see you again
I've been unemployed and lately banished
but these feelings I find the hardest
come back to see your sister
my chinstrap drips with tears

118

閑居寄諸弟

秋草生庭白露時　故園諸弟益相思

盡日高齋無一事　芭蕉葉上獨題詩

Written in the fall of 783 in Chuchou. Although the title suggests otherwise, Wei is still serving as magistrate — just not a very busy one. Chrysanthemums are the plants most commonly associated with autumn and also with old age. The first frost usually occurs during the solar period known as White Dew (early September), or about the time chrysanthemums begin blooming. In the last line, Wei Ying-wu recalls the calligrapher-monk Huai-su, who used banana leaves when he didn't have any paper handy. (3/6b)

Retired Living: To My Cousins

When plants in the courtyard bloom in the frost
I think about my cousins in our garden even more
all day in my fine quarters with nothing to do
I write poems on banana tree leaves

119

詣西山深師

曹溪舊弟子　何緣住此山　世有征戰事　心將流水閑
掃林驅虎出　宴坐一林間　藩守寧為重　擁騎造雲關

Written in the fall of 783 in Chuchou. The Buddhist monk Fa-shen lived south-
west of town on Langyashan. He was a follower of Zen's Sixth Patriarch, Hui-
neng (638–713), whose dharma seat was in Kuangtung Province at Paolin Temple
on the Tsaohsi River, and whose teaching of Zen was often identified with the
river. The South China tiger, now nearly extinct, was not as dangerous as its Sibe-
rian or Bengali counterparts, but it still killed people on occasion. (7/12b)

Visiting Master Shen on West Mountain

A longtime disciple of Tsaohsi
what brought you to this mountain
the world is a world at war
your mind is a tranquil stream
you chased the tigers out of the forest
meditating under the trees
how could a magistrate impress you
arriving at your cloud gate on horseback

120

懷琅邪深標二釋子

白雲埋大壑　陰崖滴夜泉　應居西石室　月照山蒼然

Written in the fall of 783 in Chuchou. Langyashan was a rambling mountain on the southwest outskirts of Chuchou. It was known for its springs and its caves, but also for the ravine through which the main trail courses. And it was especially known for Paoying, or Langya Temple. It was the most famous Buddhist monastery in the Huainan region and was halfway up the main trail. The two monks to whom this poem is addressed were Fa-shen and Tao-piao, who were responsible for the construction of the temple in the first place and with whom Wei exchanged a number of poems. (6/5a)

Thinking of Masters Shen and Piao on Langyashan

White clouds fill the great ravine
dark cliffs nourish night springs
you're in your rock cells facing west I imagine
where moonlight turns the mountain green

121

簡恒燦

室虛多涼氣　天高屬秋時　空庭夜風雨　草木曉離披

簡書日云曠　文墨誰復持　聊因遇澄靜　一與道人期

Written in the fall of 783 in Chuchou. Heng-ts'an was another Buddhist monk who lived on Langyashan and with whom Wei exchanged several poems. Chuchou still sees the remains of a typhoon or two in late summer or early fall. Although they bring a lot of rain in addition to wind, typhoons also suck all the moisture from the air, providing unparalleled views of the sky and surrounding landscape. (3/6b)

A Note to Heng-ts'an

Cool air fills my empty room
the sky is high and fall has arrived
last night a storm in my barren courtyard
this morning the remains of plants and trees
reports neglected for days
no one dealing with ink or words
it must be because of the quiet
or because I met a man of the Way

122

郡齋贈王卿

無術謬稱簡　素飧空自嗟　秋齋雨成滯　山藥寒始華

濩落人皆笑　幽獨歲逾賒　唯君出塵意　賞愛似山家

Written in the fall of 783 in Chuchou. The identity of Adjutant Wang is unknown. In other poems addressed to him, Wei only uses his title. Apparently he has been "rusticated" to Chuchou and has taken up residence on one of the hills outside the city. The *ch'iu-chai* (autumn study) would be his hut in the hills. The wild yam is a staple of every hermit. Near the end of chapter 1 in *Chuangtzu*, the Taoist sage chides a man for complaining about the uselessness of gourds that are too big for containers. Chuang-tzu suggests he could use them as boats. Wei's own "hermit years" were those he spent from 779 to 781 at Shanfu Temple on the Feng River. (3/6a)

From the Magistrate's Study: To Adjutant Wang

Your artlessness is wrongly called careless
I sigh in vain while eating for free
rain blocks the way to your autumn study
but wild yams don't bloom until it's cold
everyone laughs at a gigantic gourd
my own hermit years grow ever more faint
I applaud your plan of transcending the dust
of enjoying life as a mountain recluse

123

寄暢當

寇賊起東山　英俊方未閑　聞君新應募　籍籍動京關
出身文翰場　高步不可攀　青袍未及解　白羽插腰間
昔為瓊樹枝　今有風霜顏　秋郊細柳道　走馬一夕還
大夫當為國　破敵如摧山　何必事州府　坐使鬢毛班

Written in the fall of 783 in Chuchou. Ch'ang Tang was a well-known, albeit minor, poet of the mid-T'ang who volunteered to help defend the capital from a mutiny among forces passing through the Ch'ang-an area on their way to fight against the rebellions that arose in the east and northeast. The leader of the mutiny, Chu Tz'u, forced the court to flee and even declared a new dynasty. It wasn't until the following summer that the court was able to defeat the rebels and return to Ch'ang-an. Blue robes were worn by officials of the two lowest ranks. The "white feathers" are those of arrows. Wei Ying-wu aims the last couplet at himself; he regrets being of so little use in the court's defense. (3/6b)

To Ch'ang Tang

Bandit armies rose in the mountains to the east
giving our heroic men no rest
I heard you recently answered the call
the news of which stirred the capital
born into the world of letters
with attainments beyond others' reach
you didn't take off your blue robe
before hanging white feathers at your waist
you looked like a tree of jade in the past
you must be well weathered by now
down narrow lanes in the fall countryside
racing your horse to get back by dark
a true man fights for his country
knocks down mountains to defeat its foes
why must I serve as a magistrate
watching my hair turn white in vain

124

登樓寄王卿

踏閣攀林恨不同　楚雲滄海思無窮
數家砧杵秋山下　一郡荊榛寒雨中

Written in the early winter of 783 in Chuchou. Councillor Wang visited Wei in Chuchou but has since returned to Ch'ang-an. Chuchou was once in the eastern part of the ancient state of Ch'u, the name of which means "brambles." People beat clothes with mallets in fall to flatten the fabric in preparation for winter. (3/6b)

254

Climbing a Tower: To Councillor Wang

I hate climbing mountains and towers without you
the clouds and sea of Ch'u and memories never end
the sound of mallets at the foot of leafless hills
in a prefecture of brambles and winter rain

答崔都水

亭亭心中人　迢迢居秦關
憶在澧郊時　攜手望秋山
終年不事業　寢食長慵頑
攝衣辭田里　華簪耀頹顏
牧人本無術　命至苟復遷
郡齋有佳月　園林含清泉
覽君陳跡遊　詞意俱悽妍
吮稅況重疊　公門極熬煎
勿猒守窮轍　慎為名所牽

常緘素札去　適枉華章還
久嫌官府勞　初喜罷秩閑
不知為時來　名籍挂郎間
卜居又依仁　日夕正追攀
離念積歲序　歸途眇山川
同心不在宴　罇酒徒盈前
忽忽已終日　將酬不能宣
責逋甘首免　歲晏當歸田

Written in the winter of 783 in Chuchou. Wei is replying to a letter from his brother-in-law, Ts'ui Cho, who was serving as director of waterworks in Ch'ang-an. The T'ang capital was located within the boundaries of the ancient state of Ch'in. Thus, the Hanku Pass through which travelers had to go was also known as Ch'in Pass. In the first part of the poem, Wei recalls the time he lived at Shanfu Temple beside the Feng River—and where Ts'ui visited him from time to time. At the very end, he can think of nothing more to say except to remark how hard it is administering policies that cause so much suffering and to offer some pithy advice. (5/9b)

In Reply to Director Ts'ui

Man of my heart standing alone
beyond Ch'in Pass so far away
I've sent you my simple letters
your brocade response has arrived
recalling those Feng River days
arm in arm gazing at autumn hills
bored with government work
I was newly enamored of unemployed living
I did nothing productive all year
I slept and ate and couldn't have been lazier
so I don't know why it happened
my name was listed at court
I put on my robe and said goodbye to the farmers
my fancy hatpin lit up my sad face
I found a residence thanks to your kindness
I followed you around day and night
but a public servant without any skills
I was destined to be sent off again
thoughts of our separation increase with the season
I squint at the road home over mountains and rivers
even with a beautiful moon above my quarters
and a transparent spring in the garden
my heart's companion doesn't share my pleasure
I fill the wine cup before me in vain
and read your account of our wanderings
your expressions so perfectly lovely
I've been in a daze all day
and lack the words to reply
taxes are heavier and more frequent
my office is completely overwhelmed
I reprimand debtors and forgive first offenders
and let them go home at year's end
don't complain that your prospects are poor
beware the temptation of fame

宿永陽寄璨律師

遙知郡齋夜　凍雪封松竹　時有山僧來　懸燈獨自宿

Written in the winter of 783. Yungyang was the county immediately northeast of Chuchou. Since it was part of his administrative responsibility, Wei went there on government business and spent the night in the quarters set aside for officials. This poem is addressed to the Buddhist monk Heng-ts'an, who specialized in the Vinaya, or rules governing monastic and lay behavior. Heng-ts'an is spending the night in Wei's government residence back in Chuchou, but spending the night alone—as celibacy was strictly observed by Buddhist monks and nuns. Perhaps the two had planned to meet that night, but Wei was called away. Wei has several other poems to the same monk. (3/8b)

Spending the Night in Yungyang: To Vinaya Master Ts'an

I imagine this night in the magistrate's quarters
the pines and bamboos encased in snow
a mountain monk stopping to visit
hanging up his lantern sleeping alone

127

始建射侯

男子本懸弧　有志在四方
賓登時事畢　諸將備戎裝
曾習鄒魯學　亦陪鴛鷺翔

虎竹忝明命　熊侯始張皇
星飛的屢破　皷譟武更揚
一朝願投筆　世難激中腸

Written in the winter of 783 in Chuchou. With the rebel forces of Chu Tz'u occupying the capital, magistrates loyal to the emperor were ordered to prepare to defend their administrative areas, which included practicing their martial skills, such as they were. In ancient times, when a boy was born, a bow was hung outside the family's doorway to announce the auspicious occasion. On the third day, an archer would be invited to shoot arrows into the four directions as well as into the sky above and the earth below, indicating the limitless reach of the boy's future. Tallies featuring a bronze tiger and sections of bamboo were used in transmitting military orders. Archery targets often featured a painting of an animal instead of a human torso. (8/12a)

Setting Up the Archery Target for the First Time

For a son we hang up a bow
for ambition in all directions
bamboo and tiger commands have arrived
a bear target alarms us all
the time for entertaining is over
the generals have put on their armor
like meteors they hit their marks
drums make it sound more martial
I followed the Confucian path
and joined the mandarins' ranks
but one day I hope to put down my brush
such hard times wrench my insides

128

京師叛亂寄諸弟

弱冠遭世難　二紀猶未平　羇離官遠郡　虎豹滿西京
上懷犬馬戀　下有骨肉情　歸去在何時　流淚忽霑纓
憂來上北樓　左右但軍營　函谷行人絕　淮南春草生
鳥鳴野田間　思憶故園行　何當四海晏　甘與齊民耕

Written in the spring of 784 in Chuchou. A circuit refers to the length of time it takes Jupiter to circle the zodiac: twelve years. The sons of officials and nobles were "capped" when they reached the age of twenty. For Wei, this would have been in 756, or twenty-eight years earlier. Thus, the figure of twenty-four years is approximate. Ch'ang-an was also referred to as the Western Capital and Loyang as the Eastern Capital. The road that connected the two went through the Hanku Pass. Chinese officials tied their hats on with two strings, which they joined under their chins. (3/7a)

With the Capital in Chaos: To My Cousins

I was newly capped when hard times began
two circuits later we're still not at peace
an itinerant official I guard a distant district
while tigers roam the Western Capital
those above are concerned about their pets
those of us below worry about our families
I wonder if I'll ever go home
my hat strings are soaked with tears
feeling anxious I climbed North Tower
military camps stretched east and west
Hanku Pass is closed to travelers
but here in Huainan spring plants are back
birds are singing in the countryside
and I recall walking in our garden
when will the Four Seas be still
I'd be happy just to plow beside farmers

129

贈琮公

山僧一相訪　吏案正盈前

暮春華池宴　清夜高齋眠

出處似殊致　喧靜兩皆禪

此道本無得　寧復有忘筌

Written in the spring of 784 in Chuchou. The man to whom Wei wrote this poem was a Buddhist monk. Most likely he lived on nearby Langyashan. The last couplet refers to the line in *Chuangtzu*: 26 that advises forgetting the trap once the fish is caught. While it was common during the T'ang to use the words *Tao* and *Dharma* interchangeably, Wei is referring to the Tao of Confucius. (3/7b)

For Master Tsung

Ever since the master's visit
paperwork has piled up on my desk
getting away takes a special occasion
but noise and quiet are both Zen
relaxing by the garden pond in late spring
sleeping on a clear night in my lofty quarters
I can't catch a thing with this Tao
I'd be better off forgetting the trap

130

寄李儋元錫

去年花裏逢君別　今日花開已一年
世事茫茫難自料　春愁黯黯獨成眠
身多疾病思田里　邑有流亡愧俸錢
聞道欲來相問訊　西樓望月幾迴圓

Written in the spring of 784 in Chuchou. Li Tan was a palace historian and Yuan Hsi was also assigned to the court. Both men visited Wei at different times in Chuchou during the previous year. The city's West Tower looked out on the road that led back to the capital. But the capital was at this time occupied by the rebel forces of Chu Tz'u. The refugees were dislocated from towns and farms farther north during the battles along the upper reaches of the Huai River between T'ang forces and Li Hsi-lieh. Li was one of the many governors who rebelled against central authority in the aftermath of the An Lu-shan Rebellion (755–759). (3/7a)

To Li Tan and Yuan Hsi

We met and parted last year among flowers
a year later they're blooming again
human affairs are too uncertain to predict
spring is so depressing I fall asleep alone
illness plagues my body but my thoughts are in the fields
I'm ashamed of my salary with refugees in town
I heard you were planning to come for a visit
how many moons have I watched from West Tower

131

寄諸弟

歲暮兵戈亂京國　帛書間道訪存亡
還信忽從天上落　唯知彼此淚千行

Written in the summer of 784 in Chuchou. In a note to this poem, Wei says he
sent a messenger to the T'ang court at its temporary headquarters in Fengtien in
the tenth month of 783, along with letters to his family and friends. The messen-
ger returned in the fifth month of 784. (3/7b)

To My Cousins

Late last year when the capital was being looted
I sent letters by back roads to see if you survived
your answer has suddenly fallen from the sky
all we know of each other are a thousand streams of tears

132

種藥

好讀神農書　多識藥草名
不改幽澗色　宛如此地生
陰穎夕房斂　陽條夏花明
州民自寡訟　養閑非政成

持縑購山客　移蒔羅眾英
汲井既蒙澤　插檻亦扶傾
悅懌從茲始　日夕繞庭行

Written in the summer of 784 in Chuchou. Shen-nung was a legendary ruler who lived over four thousand years ago and who is credited with identifying which plants were edible and which plants had medicinal value. When texts on medicinal plants were first compiled two thousand years later, they were often attributed to him. One of the primary sources of income for hermits is the collection and sale of medicinal plants to herb collectors who then sell them in town. (8/9b)

Planting Herbs

I love reading Shen-nung's book
learning the names of plants
I buy them in bunches from herb collectors
then I transplant them and display their flowers
their mountain colors remain unchanged
as if they grew right here
I keep them moist with well water
and prop them up with stakes
I collect seeds at dusk from their shaded stalks
and flowers in summer from their sunlit branches
since I began finding pleasure in this
I walk through the courtyard day and night
and people have brought fewer cases
but my pursuit of leisure isn't office-related

133

寄恒燦

心絶去來緣　跡斷人間事　獨尋秋草徑　夜宿寒山寺
今日郡齋閑　思問楞伽字

Written in the fall of 784 in Chuchou. Heng-ts'an was a monk who lived at Langya Temple on Langyashan and with whom Wei exchanged a number of poems. The *Lankavatara Sutra* was the text used for instruction by early Zen masters in China. Its primary teaching is that all thoughts and things are nothing but mind and any division between thinker and thought is illusory. (3/7b)

To Heng-ts'an

My thoughts were free of past and future
I left the affairs of this world behind
I followed a path through autumn grass
and spent the night at a cold mountain temple
back in my quarters with nothing to do
I'm thinking of asking about the *Lankavatara*

134

寄全椒山中道士

今朝郡齋冷　忽念山中客　澗底束荊薪　歸來煮白石

欲持一瓢酒　遠慰風雨夕　落葉滿空山　何處尋行跡

Written in the fall of 784 in Chuchou. Chuanchiao Mountain was thirty kilometers south of Chuchou and within the administrative area of which Wei was magistrate. The mountain is still known today as the place where the Taoist lived to whom this poem was written. The white rocks here refer to calcium and magnesium silicates (known as actinolite) used in Chinese medicine and Taoist elixirs. (3/8a)

To the Taoist on Chuanchiao Mountain

This morning my quarters were so cold
I suddenly thought of my friend in the mountains
gathering firewood down by the creek
lugging it back to boil white rocks
I wish I could bring him a gourd full of wine
to drive off the wind and rain at night
but fallen leaves cover the deserted slopes
and how could I find the trail

135

登樓

茲樓日登眺　流歲暗蹉跎　坐厭淮南守　秋山紅樹多

Written in the fall of 784 in Chuchou. My guess is West Tower, which was where the road back to the center of the universe began and which also looked out on Langyashan to the southwest. The administrative district of Huainan, in which Chuchou was located, included all the land between the Huai River to the north and the Yangtze to the south and between the Yellow Sea in the east and the Han River in the west. (7/5a)

Climbing a Tower

I climb this tower every day and look out
at the passing years slipping into darkness
right now I'm sick of this post in Huainan
and all the red trees in these autumn hills

聞鴈

故園眇何處 歸思方悠哉 淮南秋雨夜 高齋聞鴈來

Written in the fall of 784 in Chuchou. Thoughts are going north, geese are heading south. (8/12a)

Hearing Wild Geese

My old garden is somewhere in the distance
thoughts of going home never cease
on a rainy fall night in Huainan
from my quarters upstairs I hear geese

餌黃精

靈藥出西山　服食採其根　九蒸換凡骨　經著上世言
候火起中夜　馨香滿南軒　齋君感眾靈　藥術啟妙門
自懷物外心　豈與俗士論　終期脫印綬　永與天壤存

Written in the fall of 784 in Chuchou. Solomon's seal, or *Polygonatum officianale*, is a plant whose rhizome is collected in the fall. It is used in Chinese medicine, but it's also used by Taoists to lighten the body and extend one's years. "Hills to the west" refers to Langyashan in the southwest outskirts of Chuchou. The preparation has been ritualized to emphasize the *yang* (male) energy: steam it nine times, but not before midnight, and in a room facing south, and fast before ingesting. Becoming one with Heaven and Earth, with the forces of *yin* and *yang*, is the goal of the Taoist regimen. A few months after he wrote this poem, Wei took his own advice and resigned—if only for a while. We don't see this yearning so explicitly stated in his poems very often, but clearly Wei hoped to follow a spiritual path at some point in his life. I presume he didn't because of his sense of responsibility: to maintain his family's reputation for public service and to help the people under his care. (8/7b)

Eating Solomon's Seal

This magic herb from the hills to the west
for the edible part I use the root
steaming nine times transforms it
this is what the old texts say
I tend the fire beginning at midnight
its fragrance fills my south-facing study
fasting brings out its powers
herbal arts unlock the mysteries
the thoughts I cherish of transcendence
aren't something I discuss with worldly people
someday I plan to give up this career
and live forever with Heaven and Earth

138

歲日寄京師諸季端武等

獻歲抱深慽　僑居念歸緣　常患親愛離　始覺世務牽
少事河陽府　晚守淮南壖　平生幾會散　已及蹉跎年
昨日罷符竹　家貧遂留連　部曲多已散　車馬不復全
閑將酒為偶　默以道自詮　聽松南巖寺　見月西澗泉
為政無異術　當責豈望遷　終理來時裝　歸鑿杜陵田

Written on the first day of 785 in Chuchou. Hoyang was where Wei first served as an official, albeit a very minor one, in 758. South Cliff (Nanyen) Temple was where Wei lived after resigning as magistrate of Chuchou. West Creek was just west of Chuchou and was also known as Black Sand River. The Tuling Plateau southeast of Ch'ang-an was where Wei's family home was located. It was also where his cousins were living. But going home to join them remained a lifelong wish he never seemed able to fulfill. (3/9b)

New Year's Day: To My Cousins, Including Tuan and Wu, in the Capital

With deep disappointment I face the year
an émigré wondering how to get home
troubled to be apart from those I love
feeling the drag of a worldly career
I served in Hoyang when I was young
in old age I'm guarding the shores of Huainan
how many times have we parted this life
and now we've reached our useless years
yesterday I turned in my seal of office
but poverty has forced me to stay
most of the battalions have left
and transport is in poor supply
now that I'm retired drink is my companion
I cultivate the Tao in silence
I listen to the pines at South Cliff Temple
and watch the moon along West Creek
there's no secret to government work
just do your job and don't expect a transfer
I'm finally packing the clothes I brought
I'm going home to work those Tuling fields

139

示全真元常

余辭郡符去　爾為外事牽　寧知風雪夜　復此對床眠
始話南池飲　更詠西樓篇　無將一會易　歲月坐推遷

Written in the spring of 785 in Chuchou. Although Wei had resigned as magistrate, he continued to live in Chuchou at Nanyen Temple, just outside town. The two men to whom he addresses this poem were his nephews on his wife's side and apparently visited him on a previous occasion. (3/9a)

For Ch'uan-chen and Yuan-ch'ang

I quit my post as magistrate
something else lured you here
how could I know on a snowy night
you would be lying across from me again
talking about South Lake parties
chanting West Tower poems
don't trade such times for anything
the months and years go by so fast

140

簡盧陟

可憐白雪曲　未遇知音人
恓惶戎旅下　蹉跎淮海濱
澗樹含朝雨　山鳥哢餘春
我有一瓢酒　可以慰風塵

Written in the spring of 785 in Chuchou. "White Snow" is the name of a famous tune for the zither that even in ancient times few knew how to play. The reference to this tune in the second line was to Po Ya and Chung Ch'i. Po Ya was a zither player, and Chung Ch'i (aka Chung Tzu-ch'i) was the one man who knew what was in Po Ya's heart when he played. The phrase *chih-yin* (to know one's tune) has since become a synonym for the most intimate of friends. The use of such references here suggests that Lu She has not met with a deep understanding from others — nor has Wei Ying-wu. Lu She was Wei Ying-wu's nephew. Apparently he was assigned to a military unit on a mission in the Yangchou area, and Wei was trying to encourage a visit to Chuchou. The phrase *Huai-hai* (Huai Ocean) was another name for Yangchou, which was located where the Grand Canal intersects the Yangtze and which was the administrative headquarters for the area of which Chuchou was a part. (3/10a)

Note to Lu She

You still haven't met someone who knows
the touching tune White Snow
I worry about you on the march
stumbling along Huaihai shores
streamside trees are clinging to morning rain
wild birds are singing in what is left of spring
I have a gourd of wine so big
it will wash away the dust of the road

141

西澗即事示盧陟

寢扉臨碧澗　晨起澹忘情　空林細雨至　圓文遍水生
永日無餘事　山中伐木聲　知子塵喧久　暫可散煩纓

Written in the spring of 785 in Chuchou. Wei is living in retirement at Nanyen Temple and is trying to encourage his nephew to request a leave of absence and come for a visit. Officials had to wear a hat at all times. Hence, to loosen one's hat strings means to put aside official decorum. (3/10a)

Events on West Stream: For Lu She

My bedroom door overlooks a jade stream
the stillness of dawn drives cares away
a fine rain reaches deserted woods
ripples spread across the water
nothing else happens all day
in the mountains the sound of an ax
you've lived amid dust and noise too long
come loosen those troublesome hat strings awhile

142

遊溪

野水煙鶴唳　楚天雲雨空

落花飄旅衣　歸流澹輕風

翫舟清景晚　垂釣綠蒲中

緣源不可極　遠樹但青蔥

Written in the spring of 785. Wei was boating on a river near Chuchou. In the background is the story made famous by T'ao Yuan-ming about a fisherman who traces peach petals upstream and discovers them coming from a hidden world where people live in peace. But after returning to his village to tell others, the fisherman is unable to find the way there again. (7/9b)

Boating on a River

Cranes called through the spray of surging waters
Ch'u skies were free of clouds and rain
at the end of a quiet day of boating
I was fishing among green rushes
when petals landed on my outdoor robe
a light breeze was blowing upstream
as I worked my way to their unreachable source
among distrant trees I saw a hint of green

PART FOUR

Chiangchou & Suchou

(785–791)/33 poems

143

始至郡

溢城古雄郡　橫江千里馳　高樹上迢遞　峻蝶繞欹危
井邑煙火晚　郊原草樹滋　洪流蕩北阯　崇嶺鬱南圻
斯民本樂生　逃逝竟何為　早歲屬荒歉　舊逋積如坻
到郡方逾月　終朝理亂絲　賓朋未及醵　簡牘已云疲
昔賢播高風　得守媿無施　豈待干戈戢　且願撫惸嫠

Written in the late summer of 785, not long after Wei reached his new post as magistrate of Chiangchou. The city's modern name is Chiuchiang, or Nine Rivers. Since the city was built where one of those rivers, namely the Pen, joins the Yangtze, it was also called Pencheng, or Pen City. Lushan, or Hut Mountain, rises a few kilometers south of town. It was once the residence of countless recluses but is now the destination of tourists. During Wei's tenure here, famines and warfare forced many people to become refugees. The worthy whom

On First Reaching This Prefecture

Pencheng is an ancient and strategic town
straddling a river that races a thousand miles
tall trees tower overhead
steep parapets wind around
neighborhoods fill with kitchen smoke at dusk
every plant and tree in the countryside is green
an ocean of water surges past the north wall
a lofty ridge rises beyond the south rampart
people here once loved life
so why have they run away
after years of drought and poor harvests
their unpaid taxes form hills
I've been in this prefecture more than a month
finally today I cleared up the mess
but acquaintances haven't come by for dinner
and I'm already bored with reports
worthies of the past rode a higher wind
I'm embarrassed to serve in a meaningless post
do I have to wait for warfare to end
before comforting widows and orphans

Wei most likely has in mind is T'ao Yuan-ming, who had the good sense to retire
from government service and live out his life as a farmer at the southeast foot of
Lushan. The warfare of concern to officials along the middle reaches of the Yang-
tze was the revolt of the separatist governor Li Hsi-lieh, who controlled most of
the western half of the Huai River watershed to the north as well as such strate-
gic waterways as the Kaifeng Canal. In line eleven, I've gone along with later edi-
tions and replaced *tsao* (early) with the nearly identical *han* (drought). (8/6a)

144

登郡樓寄京師諸季淮南子弟

始罷永陽守　復臥潯陽樓　懸檻飄寒雨　危堞侵江流
迢茲聞鴈夜　重憶別離秋　徒有盈樽酒　鎮此百端憂

Written in the fall of 785 in Chiangchou. Yungyang was another name for Chuchou, and Hsunyang was an old name for Chiangchou. The Chiangchou city wall was built along the Yangtze, and the tower on which Wei stands, which is still there, was built at the river's edge. After leaving Chuchou, Wei visited his nephews in Yangchou before sailing up the Yangtze to Chiangchou. He said goodbye to his cousins in Ch'ang-an three years earlier in the summer—but it probably felt like fall. (3/10a)

Climbing the City Tower: To My Cousins in the Capital and My Nephews in Huainan

I recently quit my post in Yungyang
and already I'm lounging in Hsunyang Tower
a cold rain spatters the balcony railing
the steep parapet juts into the Yangtze
I've heard wild geese every night since arriving
I keep recalling our autumn goodbyes
the wine in this cup doesn't work
diluted by so many cares

145

登蒲塘驛泝路見泉谷村墅忽想
京師舊居追懷昔年

青山導騎遠　春風行旆舒　均徭視屬城　問疾躬里閭
煙水依泉谷　川陸散樵漁　忽念故園日　復憶驪山居
荏苒班鬢及　夢寢婚宦初　不覺平生事　呫嗟二紀餘
存沒闊已永　悲多歡自疎　高秩非為美　闌干淚盈裾

Written in the spring of 786 while touring the counties under the jurisdiction of Chiangchou Prefecture. Putang Post Station and Chuanku Village were southwest of Lushan in what is now Te-an County. The cycle Wei refers to was one that lasted twelve years. Twenty-four years earlier would have been 762, and adding a few more to that would put Wei's recollections around 756–758: his service in the imperial guard from 751 to 756, his marriage in 756, and his first official assignment in 758. (6/6a)

Leaving Putang Post Station and Seeing the Farmsteads of Chuanku Village along the Way, I Suddenly Think of My Old Home in the Capital and Recall the Bygone Years

My guides weave through green mountains
my travel pennants flap in spring wind
adjusting corvée in outlying towns
I ask about hardships in person
Chuanku Village is all water and mist
fishermen and woodsmen dot rivers and hills
suddenly I recall days in my garden
and nights on Lishan once more
over the years my temples have turned gray
my marriage and first post are a dream
oblivious to all that has happened this life
I sigh to have lived over two cycles more
but birth and death go on forever
with sorrows too many and joys too few
a high official's life isn't so grand
look at my tear-stained robe

146

山行積雨歸塗始霽

攬轡窮登降　陰雨邁二旬　但見白雲合　不睹巖中春
急澗豈易揭　峻塗良難遵　深林猿聲冷　沮洳虎跡新
始霽升陽景　山水閟清晨　雜花積如霧　百卉萋已陳
鳴驂屢驤首　歸路自忻忻

Written in the spring of 786 while touring the counties under the jurisdiction of Chiuchiang Prefecture. While Wei is holding on to his bridle for dear life, he rides through a landscape still known today for its mists. However, the last gibbons and tigers disappeared from the Lushan area midway through the twentieth century. (6/7b)

Mounting Up to Go Back After Traveling in the Mountains in Heavy Rain

I cling to the bridle going up then down
twenty days now nothing but rain
all I see are gathering clouds
no sign of spring in the cliffs
it's not easy staying dry fording streams
and mountain trails are too hard to follow
gibbons fill the woods with their eerie howls
the tiger tracks in the mud look fresh
as we mount up the sun finally breaks through
I survey the landscape of dawn
flowers are as dense as fog
a hundred different plants surround us
our horses whinny and keep turning their heads
they're glad to be going home

147

送王校書

同宿高齋換時節　共看移石復栽杉
送君江浦已惆悵　更上西樓望遠帆

Written in the spring of 786 in Chiangchou. Wang's title suggests he was serving on the staff of the heir apparent. Wei's friend is heading up the Yangtze on his way back to the capital. Apparently, Wei was doing some landscaping in the garden attached to his new quarters. (4/11b)

Seeing Off Secretary Wang

From the fine rooms we shared as the seasons changed
we watched men moving rocks and planting fir trees
seeing you off at the river was depressing
then from West Tower I watched your sail disappear

148

寄黃劉二尊師

盧山兩道士　各在一峯居　矯掌白雲表　晞髮陽和初

清夜降真侶　焚香滿空虛　中有無為樂　自然與世疎

道尊不可屈　符守豈暇餘　高齋遙致敬　願示一編書

Written in the summer of 786 in Chiangchou. Huang Tung-yuan, fifteenth-generation master of the Maoshan Taoist lineage, was living on Lushan's Incense Burner Peak, and Liu Hsuan-ho, another Taoist master, was living on Five Worthy Peak. Despite their cultivation of seclusion, these two Taoists maintained a correspondence with a number of literary figures of the day. Taoists practice *ch'i-kung/qigong* exercises for general health and as part of their training aimed at achieving oneness with the Tao. Unlike Buddhist monks, Taoists don't cut their hair and have to wait for a sunny day to wash it. They also conduct ceremonies to call down various immortals to assist them in their practice. At the end of the poem, Wei sighs that he hasn't been able to convince the two men to come to see him, and he doesn't have time to see them. But he hopes for instruction, nevertheless. Whenever Wei moved to a new place, he made it a point to get in touch with the local masters, be they Buddhists or Taoists. (3/10b)

To Masters Huang and Liu

My two Taoist friends on Lushan
each on a different peak
moving your hands as if they were clouds
washing your hair when the weather turns warm
calling down immortals in the middle of the night
burning incense until it covers the sky
finding the joys of doing nothing up there
being natural and out of touch with the world
such masters of the Tao can't be lured down
but neither can a magistrate find time
I send my respects to your lofty retreats
and hope for a letter of instruction

149

因省風俗訪道士姪
不見題壁

去年澗水今亦流　去年杏花今又拆
山人歸來問是誰　還是去年行春客

Written at the beginning of 787 in Chiangchou. Officials were required to tour their administrative regions at the beginning of the year and observe local customs. Here, Wei visits nearby Lushan and fails to find his nephew Wei Ch'eng-hsu in his hut and leaves this poem behind. Wei wrote another poem to his nephew while the two were making a similar spring tour the previous year. In the first line, I've gone along with later editions and replaced *pu* (not) with the graphically similar *yi* (still). (5/15a)

While Observing Local Customs, I Visit My Taoist Nephew without Success and Write This on His Wall

Last year's mountain stream is still flowing today
last year's apricot blossoms I picked again today
a hermit on the trail asks me who I am
I'm the same spring visitor I was last year

150

春思

野花如雪繞江城　坐見年芳憶帝京
閭闔曉開凝碧樹　曾陪鴛鷺聽流鶯

Written in the early spring of 787 in Chiangchou. Wei recalls his days at court. Mandarin ducks refer to officials, who entered the palace in pairs wearing ornate robes. Commentators say the orioles here refer to musicians, but the singing of orioles is also a recurrent reference to those who give honest advice that goes unheeded. (6/4a)

Spring Thoughts

Snow white wildflowers surround this river town
viewing their annual blooms I recall the royal city
the palace gates at dawn opening on trees of jade
standing beside the mandarins listening to the orioles

151

寒食寄京師諸弟

把酒看花想諸弟　　杜陵寒食草青青
雨中禁火空齋冷　　江上流鶯獨坐聽

Written in the spring of 787 in Chiangchou. Cold Food was the name of a three-day period in early April when fires were forbidden. The custom goes back 2,500 years to Duke Wen of the state of Chin and commemorates the death of the hermit Chieh Chih-t'ui, who refused to come out of seclusion to serve at the duke's court. Furious at Chieh's refusal, the duke ordered the mountain on which Chieh lived set afire. Chieh still refused to come down and died in the blaze. Out of remorse, the duke banned fire every year during the three days before Grave Sweeping Day, and the custom persisted until modern times. Drinking wine and viewing the flowers of spring were once part of the celebration of Cold Food Days. A favorite spring excursion in Ch'ang-an was to hike along the Chuchiang Waterway and up to the Tuling Plateau to view the flowering fruit trees. The oriole is the bird of spring and of courtship, but T'ang poets also heard in its song complaints against government policies. (3/9b)

Cold Food Days: To My Cousins in the Capital

My empty rooms are bleak on a rainy day with fire banned
I sit alone and listen to orioles by the river
I've had the wine and seen the flowers but think about my cousins
Cold Food Days on Tuling the grass by now is green

尋簡寂觀瀑布

躡石歆危過急澗　攀崖迢遞弄懸泉
猶將虎竹為身累　欲付歸人絕世緣

Written in the spring of 787 in Chiangchou. Chienchi Temple was a Taoist her-
mitage near the southeastern end of Lushan. It was south of Chienchi Peak and
west of Changkung Ridge and was first built by the Taoist master Lu Hsiu-ching,
who settled on the mountain in 461. The waterfall Wei was looking for was along
a gorge west of the temple. (7/12b)

Looking for Chienchi Temple Waterfall

Treading precipitous rocks I cross the rushing water
and clamber up a towering cliff to enjoy a suspended stream
but seals of office still weigh my body down
if only someone took them back I could cut my worldly ties

153

題鄭弘憲侍御遺愛草堂

居士近依僧　青山結茅屋　疏松映嵐晚　春池含苔綠

繁華冒陽嶺　新禽響幽谷　長嘯攀喬林　慕茲高世躅

Written in the spring of 787 in Chiangchou. Touring Lushan, Wei visits the newly built hut of his friend Cheng Chang. Cheng's hut was just north of Incense Burner Peak. Later that spring he left on a mission from which he didn't return (cf. poem 154). Several decades later, Pai Chu-yi built his own hut just west of Cheng's old hut, which by then had become a temple of the same name: *Yi-ai-ssu* (Left Behind Love). (7/14a)

Written on Censor Cheng Hung-hsien's Left Behind Love Hut

A layman who's more like a monk
he built his hut among distant peaks
where mist shines through scattered pines at sunset
and moss fills his pond in spring with green
where a multitude of flowers blankets a sunlit ridge
and fledgling birds call across dark valleys
whistling out loud I hike past towering trees
admiring the heights his footsteps have reached

154

東林精舍見故殿中鄭侍御題詩
追舊書情涕泗橫集因寄呈閻澧
州馮少府

仲月景氣佳　東林一登歷　中有故人詩　淒涼在高壁
精思長懸世　音容已歸寂　墨澤傳灑餘　磨滅親翰跡
平生忽如夢　百事皆成昔　結騎京華年　揮文篋笥積
朝庭重英彥　時輩分珪璧　永謝柏梁陪　獨關金門籍
方嬰存沒感　豈暇林泉適　雨餘山景寒　風散花光夕
新知雖滿堂　故情誰能覯　唯當同時友　緘寄空悽感

Written in the summer of 787 when Wei visited Tunglin Temple. Tunglin was where the monk Hui-yuan once lived, and it is still the most famous temple on Lushan—although it's not actually on the mountain but at its northwestern foot. The calligraphy Wei Ying-wu sees on the temple wall is by his friend Cheng Chang (Cheng Hung-hsien). Cheng and the two men to whom he sends this poem served together with Wei in the palace guard in the 750s. Cheng was murdered during a mission in the fifth month of 787 by Wu Shao-ch'eng, one of the regional governors who refused to accept the court's authority. Among the insignia of rank used at court were tablets and disks of jade. Cedar Hall (Poliang) was an old name for that part of the palace used for entertaining officials. And officials had to pass through Bronze Horse Gate (Chinmamen) on their way to the daily predawn audience, assuming their names were on the list of those allowed inside. (6/11a)

After Seeing a Poem at Tunglin Temple Written by Former Censor and Palace Attendant Cheng Expressing His Feelings about the Past, with Tears Gathering in Both Eyes I Send This to Magistrate Yen of Fengchou and Director Feng

Midsummer and the weather was fine
and the trail led past Tunglin
inside was an old friend's poem
off by itself high on a wall
his insights once echoed throughout the realm
but his voice has now been stilled
the ink revealed a brushstroke or two
but what he had written was worn away
suddenly his life is a dream
all that he did is now past
those years we rode through the capital together
with satchels full of our latest work
the court valued our looks and our talents
and our colleagues held jade disks and tablets
but our Cedar Hall posts are gone for good
our names aren't listed at Bronze Horse Gate
entangled by thoughts of life and death
how can I relax among forests and streams
the mountain feels chilly after a rain
the wind scatters flowers in the fading light
new acquaintances fill my hall
but where can I find my old companion
it's only to friends who shared those days
I can seal and send this useless lament

155

西寒山

勢從千里奔　直入江中斷　嵐橫秋塞雄　地束驚流滿

Written in the fall of 787 upriver from Chiangchou. Wei was traveling up the Yangtze by boat on his way to Ch'ang-an, to which he had been recalled. Hsisai Mountain is sixty-five kilometers downstream from Wuhan, near the town of Huchou, and juts into the Yangtze from the river's south shore. There is another mountain of the same name another fifty kilometers downstream near the town of Huangshih. The name means Western Bastion and comes from the fact that both mountains stood at the western border of the ancient state of Wu at different times. The first couplet likens the mountain to a mill wheel, sticking into and thus powered by the river. (8/11a)

Hsisai Mountain

Its power comes from this thousand-mile torrent
jutting halfway into the river
a mighty bastion barring fall with its mist
from here it controls the whole flood

156

聽嘉陵江水聲寄深上人

鑿崖泄奔湍　稱古神禹跡　夜喧山門店　獨宿不安席
水性自云靜　石中本無聲　如何兩相激　雷轉空山驚
貽之道門舊　了此物我情

Written in the fall of 787, in Szechuan Province, while traveling back to Ch'ang-an. On his way back to Ch'ang-an from Chiangchou, Wei traveled west up the Yangtze as far as Chungching and then turned north up the Chialing before reaching the Chinling Range and the final overland stage of the journey back to the capital. Master Shen was a Buddhist monk on Langyashan outside Chuchou with whom Wei became friends while serving there as magistrate. Yu the Great (c. 2200 B.C.) was the founder of the Hsia dynasty and is credited with dredging rivers to control flooding, which then made permanent agricultural settlements possible. The place that inspired this poem is located 15 kilometers south of the river town of Nanpu, or about 250 kilometers north of Chungching, on the Chialing River. (2/3b)

Listening to the Sound of Water on the Chialing River: To Master Shen

A torrent shoots through carved-out cliffs
the work of Yu the Sage they say
all night it echoed at the inn below
where I lodged alone unable to sleep
the nature of water is said to be stillness
and rocks are essentially silent
so why when these two clash
do they wake the whole mountain with thunder
I send this to my old friend of the Way
wherein you will find my feelings

157

至開化里壽春公故宅

寧知府中吏　故宅一徘徊　歷階存往敬　瞻位泣餘哀

廢井沒荒草　陰牖生綠苔　門前車馬散　非復昔時來

Written in the spring of 788 in Ch'ang-an. Upon returning to the capital, Wei was appointed director of one of the bureaus in the Department of State Affairs. Duke Shou-ch'un was the title of Wei's old friend and patron, Li Huan, who arranged for Wei to serve in Ch'ang-an Prefecture and later Huhsien County from the spring of 774 through the summer of 779. Li was later executed on charges of corruption. The Kaihua Quarter was just south of the Forbidden City's South Gate. During the T'ang, people normally sat on mats either on the floor or on a raised platform. The use of chairs was not widespread until after the T'ang dynasty. (6/11b)

Visiting Duke Shou-ch'un's Old Home in the Kaihua Quarter

Serving at the prefecture I never guessed
I would be lingering at your old home
walking up the steps I felt the same respect
but when I saw your seat my tears turned to sobs
the abandoned well buried beneath weeds
the darkened windows covered with moss
carts and horses are gone from the gate
and those days won't come again

158

送馮著受李廣州署為錄事

鬱鬱楊柳枝　蕭蕭征馬悲
送君灞陵岸　糾郡南海湄
名在翰墨場　羣公正追隨
如何從此去　千里萬里朝
大海吞東南　橫嶺隔地維
建邦臨日域　溫燠御四時
百國共臻湊　珍奇獻京師
富豪虞興戎　繩墨不易持
州伯荷天寵　還當翊丹墀
子為門下生　終始豈見遺
所願酌貪泉　心不為磷緇
上將酧國士　下以報渴飢

Written in the late spring or early summer of 788 in Ch'ang-an. In 787 Li Fu was appointed magistrate of Kuangchou (Canton) and governor of the region of which that city was the administrative center. Some commentators mistake Li Fu for Li Mien, who was appointed magistrate of Kuangchou in 769. But Wei was in Loyang from 763 until 774, and this poem was clearly written in Ch'ang-an. The Pa River, just east of Ch'ang-an, was a favorite place to say goodbye, where it was a custom to break off a willow catkin as a present to the departing friend:

Seeing Off Feng Chu upon His Appointment as Adjutant to Li Kuang-chou

Ah the glorious willow catkins
and the mournful whinnies of a traveler's horse
seeing you off beside the Pa River
off to inspect our South Sea precincts
your name resounds in literary circles
where others trail behind you
what takes you so far away
on a trip of a thousand no ten thousand miles
where the Great Sea swallows the southeast coast
and the High Ranges bar the ends of the earth
where the ramparts overlook the home of the sun
and hot weather lasts all year
where envoys arrive from a hundred lands
bringing tribute and treasure for the throne
where the wealthy worry about insurrections
and rules of conduct aren't easy to uphold
but the Prefect enjoys Heaven's favor
and still assists on cinnabar steps
and you are his disciple
so how could this be exile
but if you should drink from the Spring of Greed
may your heart not be corrupted
and may you report to the one above
on the hunger and thirst of those below

the word for willow, *liu*, was a homophone for another word that meant "stay." Feng Chu was an old friend who had previously failed to gain the good graces of those who handed out appointments. But his fortunes had changed, and he was now leaving to take up an appointment as adjutant to a favorite of the court. The "cinnabar steps" were inside the palace where the predawn audience with the emperor was held. There was a spring in Kuangchou called the Spring of Greed, whose water promised wealth to those who drank it. (4/4b)

159

送李侍御益赴幽州幕

二十揮篇翰　三十窮典墳　辟書五府至　名為四海聞
始從車騎幕　今赴嫖姚軍　契闊晚相遇　草感遽離羣
悠悠行子遠　眇眇川塗分　登高望燕代　日夕生夏雲
司徒擁精甲　誓將除國氛　儒生幸持斧　可以佐功勳
無言羽書急　坐闕相思文

Written in the summer of 788 in Ch'ang-an. Yuchou was the name of a T'ang-dynasty province centered around Beijing. This area was also controlled by the ancient state of Yen. In order to reach Yen (or Yuchou), most travelers from Ch'ang-an arrived from the west via the passes controlled by the ancient state of Tai. Li Yi (b. 748) was a member of a prominent family and was sent to Yuchou to represent the court on the staff of the governor, Liu Chi, who the court was hoping would lead his forces against other more rebellious governors in the central plains. (4/10b)

Seeing Off Censor Li Yi to the Yuchou Field Command

At twenty you brandished books and a pen
by thirty you exhausted the classics
then your appointment to the garrison arrived
and your name was heard through the land
at first you served at cavalry headquarters
now you're off to join the Whirlwind Army
cutting short our evening together
in such a great hurry to leave
a son traveling far from home
where rivers and roads part in the distance
looking down on Yen and Tai from the heights
where summer clouds rise morning and night
your governor possesses the best of forces
and has vowed to rid the stench from the nation
and my lucky friend holds the ax of a censor
perfect for assisting in a worthy service
but don't say you're busy with reports
and stop writing your friends

160

寄二嚴

絲竹久已懶　今日遇君忺

打破蜘蛛千道網　總為鶺鴒兩箇嚴

Written in the summer of 788 in Ch'ang-an. This poem is somewhat irregular: two five-character lines, followed by two seven-character lines. The original edition includes a note that identifies the two men to whom this poem was addressed as Yen Shih-liang, magistrate of Wuchou (Chekiang Province), and Yen Shih-yuan, magistrate of Pingchou (Hunan Province). Both men resigned their posts, and Wei wishes he could do the same. The (pied) wagtail is a bird known for its devotion to its siblings. Once again, we can only wonder why Wei did not sever that same web. (3/12a)

To the Two Yens

Flute and zither have lately bored me
but meeting you today I'm pleased
knowing you two wagtail Yens
have severed the thousand-strand spiderweb

161

雪後下朝呈省中
一絕

南望青山滿禁闈　曉陪鴛鷺正差池
共愛朝來何處雪　蓬萊宮裏拂松枝

Written in the winter of 788 in Ch'ang-an. The ridges visible to the south were
those of the Chungnan Mountains. Penglai Palace was another name for Taming
Palace and the scene of the morning audience, which Wei was required to attend
as a senior member in the Department of State Affairs. Nothing like a little snow
to melt court decorum. (2/12b)

Leaving Court after a Snowfall: A Quatrain for Those in the Department of State Affairs

Dark mountains to the south filled forbidden gates
we stood at dawn with mandarins in uneven ranks
so happy to see snow wherever we looked
at Penglai Palace we shook the pine branches

162

閶門懷古

獨鳥下高樹　遙知吳苑園　淒涼千古事　日暮倚閶門

Written in the spring of 789 shortly after he arrived in Suchou to serve as magistrate. Changmen Gate was an old name for Suchou's West Gate. This was the gate from which the armies of the ancient state of Wu marched during the first millennium B.C. Suchou was the capital of Wu, until the arrogance, ignorance, and indulgence of its king, Fu Ch'a, resulted in Wu's annihilation. The gardens of Suchou that Fu Ch'a and his concubine, Hsi Shih, enjoyed were between the city and Lake Taihu to the south. But the city was home to dozens of elaborate gardens in succeeding dynasties as well, and still is. Wei combines here the history of the state of Wu, the T'ang dynasty, and his own life. (6/12a)

Thinking of the Past at Changmen Gate

A lone bird lands on a towering tree
having heard from afar of the gardens of Wu
lamenting the history of a thousand years
at sunset I lean against Changmen Gate

163

夏至避暑北池

晝晷已云極　宵漏自此長

未及施政教　所憂變炎涼

公門日多暇　是月農稍忙

高居念田里　苦熱安可當

亭午息羣物　獨遊愛方塘

門閉陰寂寂　城高樹蒼蒼

綠筠尚含粉　圓荷始散芳

於焉洒煩抱　可以對華觴

Written in the fifth month of 789 in Suchou. Humid summer weather still plagues the Yangtze Delta, where people look for a place to escape the heat whenever they can. North Lake was located at the back of Yungting Temple and is part of what is now called West Garden. The Chinese used a variety of instruments to measure the sun's shadow as well as a variety of devices that dripped water to measure the passage of time at night. (7/13b)

Escaping the Heat at North Lake at the Beginning of Summer

The sundial has reached its limit
the waterclock begins dripping longer tonight
my official instructions haven't arrived
I'm more concerned about the change in the weather
though I'm invariably free at the office
farmers this month are busy
living in comfort I think of them toiling
and wonder how they deal with the heat
creatures all rest at midday
I alone love to visit this lake
the gate is closed it's shady and quiet
the walls are high and the trees are dense
the new bamboo looks powdery-green
and lotuses are starting to send forth perfume
but how shall I soothe a troubled heart
perhaps with a jug of good wine

164

郡齋雨中與諸文士燕集

兵衛森畫戟　宴寢凝清香　海上風雨至　逍遙池閣涼
煩痾近消散　嘉賓復滿堂　自慙居處崇　未覩斯民康
理會是非遺　性達形跡忘　鮮肥屬時禁　蔬果幸見嘗
俯飲一杯酒　仰聆金玉章　神歡體自輕　意欲凌風翔
吳中盛文史　羣彥今汪洋　方知大藩地　豈曰財賦疆

Written in the summer of 789, a month or two after his arrival in Suchou. Government offices were allowed to have a certain number of armed guards painted along their walls depending on their status in the bureaucratic hierarchy. The troubles Wei refers to as having been dispelled concerned rebellious provinces. But even after they were brought under control, they rebelled again. Among the literati present at this banquet was Ku K'uang, who had stopped here in his hometown on his way into exile. This poem had a great impact at the time, and it resulted in poems in response not only by Ku K'uang but also by Liu T'ai-chen,

Gathering at the Magistrate's Hall in the Rain for a Banquet with the Literati

Military guards and rows of painted halberds
the purest of perfumes in the inner rooms
and wind and rain fresh from the sea
cooling the lakeside pavilion where we lounge
troubles and ills have lately been dispersed
noble guests fill the hall once more
I'm embarrassed to live in such splendor
having yet to examine the condition of the people
but understanding reason we banish right and wrong
understanding life we transcend the world of form
despite the seasonal ban on fish and meat
vegetables and fruits are ours to enjoy
we bend down and drink cups of wine
we look up and hear noble words
with our spirits pleased and our bodies relaxed
our hopes soar on the breeze
the history of letters in the land of Wu is rich
its accomplished scholars are legion
now that I've seen this tributary state
how can I call it the Revenue Frontier

Fang Ju-fu (who was serving as magistrate of Hangchou), and Wei Ts'an. Such was its fame that when Pai Chu-yi became magistrate of Suchou thirty-some years later, he had this poem carved on a stele. The government decreed a ban on hunting and butchering during the fifth lunar month, beginning in 785, to allow animal populations to recover. The area administered from Suchou, which was once the capital of the ancient state of Wu, was the single greatest source of revenue for the central government. (1/8b)

165

秋夜寄丘二十二員外

懷君屬秋夜

散步詠涼天

山空松子落

幽人應未眠

Written in the fall of 789 in Suchou. Ch'iu Tan had served briefly as Wei's secretary. His title here suggests he had been appointed to a post beyond the quota permitted and would therefore receive only half the allotted salary. Ch'iu decided he would rather cultivate the Tao. He quit his post, crossed the Yangtze, and retired to a hermitage on Pingshan, just outside the northwest gate of Yangchou. Pingshan was also the location of Taming Temple. Several decades earlier, the Buddhist monk Chien-chen left this temple and traveled to Japan, where he is

Autumn Night: To Supernumerary Ch'iu Twenty-two

Out walking and singing of cooler days
I think of you on this autumn night
pinecones falling on deserted slopes
the recluse I suspect not yet asleep

credited with introducing the Vinaya school of Buddhism and Chinese medicine to the Japanese. Thus, the slopes of Pingshan, which was not a large mountain, were not exactly deserted. Still, this was the eighth full moon, or the Mid-Autumn Festival, when relatives and friends normally spend the night together, and Wei tries to imagine how lonely his friend must feel. Pinecones remain an important source of food for recluses in China, but here Wei uses them to emphasize Ch'iu Tan's isolation. (3/10b)

166

九日

一為吳郡守　不覺菊花開　始有故園思　且喜眾賓來

Written on the ninth day of the ninth month of 789 in Suchou. Wei has another poem by this title, which begins this book. Wu Prefecture was another name for Suchou, as it was once the capital of the state of Wu. This poem was added to the *Weisuchouchi* edition around 1170.

The Ninth

Suddenly I'm governing Wu Prefecture
and suddenly chrysanthemums are blooming
as I start to think of my garden back home
happily a group of guests arrives

167

聽江笛送陸侍御

遠聽江上笛 臨觴一送君 還愁獨宿夜 更向郡齋聞

Written in the early winter of 789 in Suchou. Censor Lu, or Lu Ts'an, was a native of Suchou, but he was stationed in Shaohsing and was returning to his post via the Grand Canal. Ch'iu Tan, Wei's former secretary, also wrote a poem to Lu on the same occasion. (4/12b)

Hearing a Flute on the River After Seeing Off Censor Lu

Seeing you off over cups of wine
in the distance I heard a flute on the river
spending the night alone is sad enough
without hearing it again in my quarters

168

軍中冬燕

滄海已云晏
皇恩猶念勤
式燕偏恆秩
柔遠及斯人
茲邦實大藩
伐鼓軍樂陳
是時冬服成
戎士氣益振
虎竹謬朝寄
英賢降上賓
旋罄周旋禮
媿無海陸珍
庭中丸劍闌
堂上鼓吹新
光景不知晚
魷酌豈言頻
單醪昔所感
大醸況同忻
顧謂軍中士
仰答何由申

Written in the winter of 789 in Suchou. A number of regional warlords had been defeated or made peace, and the central government ordered banquets throughout the realm to thank those who took part in defending its interests. Note that the ban on fish and meat is still in effect for such an occasion. Apparently it was extended beyond the fifth lunar month. (1/9a)

A Winter Banquet for the Army

Turbulent seas have been calmed
the throne remembers those who helped
a banquet in honor of all career soldiers
a kindness to those from far and near
this is the greatest of tributaries
so beat the drums and array the musicians
with winter clothes now ready
our officers' valor grows stronger
my orders mistook the court's intent
asking heroes and worthies to bow to old men
as soon as they're done the ceremony starts
alas without dishes from land or sea
but the courtyard is alive with martial games
and the songs on the stage are new
for such an occasion it's never late
how often can we hoist a ram's horn
a single cup brings thoughts of the past
a big jug means more pleasure all around
looking at these men in the army
I wonder how to thank the throne

169

遊開元精舍

夏衣始輕體　遊步愛僧居

綠陰生晝靜　孤花表春餘

果園新雨後　香臺照日初

符竹方為累　形跡一來疎

Written in the early summer of 790. In 738, Emperor Hsuan-tsung ordered every prefecture and city in the empire to name a monastery within its jurisdiction Kaiyuan, after his reign title. This particular Kaiyuan Temple was south of Suchou. Such was the fame of this poem that one of the temple's buildings was later renamed Green Shade Hall. (7/9b)

Visiting Kaiyuan Hermitage

As soon as I feel the lightness of summer clothes
I love to follow trails to monastic retreats
to an orchard of fruit trees after a rain
a terrace of incense lit by the dawn
where green shade nurtures quiet days
and a solitary blossom is the last sign of spring
my official duties have kept me so busy
my footsteps have come here too seldom

登重玄寺閣

時暇陟雲構　晨躋澄景光　始見吳都大　十里鬱蒼蒼
山川表明麗　湖海吞大荒　合沓臻水陸　駢闐會四方
俗繁節又暄　雨順物亦康　禽魚各翔泳　草木遍芬芳
於茲省氓俗　一用勸農桑　誠知虎符忝　但恨歸路長

Written in the summer of 790 in Suchou. Chunghsuan Temple was a kilometer or so northwest of the city wall. It was originally built in the sixth century as a residence for a royal prince who later turned it over to monks. In the ninth century, it became famous for the carving of Buddhist sutras on rock walls. Immediately to the east was the Grand Canal, and in the distance to the west was Lake Taihu, the largest freshwater lake in China. This was one of the richest agricultural areas in China and also the biggest center of silk production—hence the mention of the mulberry trees that fed the silkworms. Officials were given one

Climbing the Pagoda at Chunghsuan Temple

On my day off I climbed into the clouds
morning rain cleared for an unobstructed view
I finally beheld the greatness of Suchou
ten *li* of flourishing green
the bright beauty of rivers and hills
a great plain swallowed by the greatest of lakes
the layered confluence of land and water
a place where the four quarters meet
a panoply of customs and happy festivals
abundant rain and plentiful crops
where fish and fowl swim and soar
and plants and trees all smell sweet
from here I can see the farmers
working in fields and mulberry groves
although I've clearly disgraced my command
I only regret the road home is so long

day off every ten days. Of course, official business could often be wrapped up well before midday, leaving officials free to take a good part of every day off. One commentator notes that upon climbing Taishan, Confucius thought the state of Lu looked small, while Wei Ying-wu climbs a pagoda and thinks Suchou huge. When Buddhist temples were first built in China, they were usually built around a stupa containing the relics of an eminent monk. As time went on, stupas became pagodas, with interior staircases and windows and even balconies on the upper stories for viewing the surrounding landscape. (7/5b)

171

答秦十四校書

知掩山扉三十秋　魚鬣翠碧弃牀頭

莫道謝公方在郡　五言今日為君休

Written in the fall of 790 in Suchou. Wei wrote this in reply to a poem from his friend Ch'in Hsi, who was a prominent poet of the time. In the aftermath of the An Lu-shan Rebellion, Ch'in took refuge on a mountain outside Shaohsing and ended up living there for thirty years. In 790, Ch'in finally accepted an appointment in Hsuchou, farther up the Grand Canal. On his way, he stopped in Suchou to see Wei and other friends. Master Hsieh refers to the famous fifth-century landscape poet Hsieh T'iao, also known as Hsieh Hsuan-hui. During his visit, Ch'in wrote, "Hsieh Hsuan-hui is now in Suchou." Hsieh was a master of the five-syllable line—in Chinese each character is one syllable and usually equivalent to what we think of as a word. But Wei was an even greater master of this form. In fact, some poets and literary critics rank him ahead of all others—Pai Chu-yi certainly did. Wei wrote this reply with seven-syllable lines. (5/12b)

In Reply to Secretary Ch'in Fourteen

Thirty autumns your mountain gate stayed closed
your regalia and seal of office tossed beneath your bed
stop saying Master Hsieh is in this district now
I'm giving up five-word lines because of you

172

答鄭騎曹青橘絕句

憐君臥病思新橘　試摘猶酸亦未黃
書後欲題三百顆　洞庭須待滿林霜

Written on the ninth day of the ninth month of 790, in Suchou. The identity of
the man to whom Wei is writing is unknown. His title only indicates he was in
charge of supplying mounts for the cavalry. The oranges for which the man longs
are a famous product of the slopes of the Tungtingshan Peninsula, just west of
Suchou on the east shore of Lake Taihu. Their flavor was said to be enhanced by
the first frost of autumn. (5/12b)

In Reply to Chief Stockman Cheng's Quatrain Requesting Oranges

I'm sorry you're ill and thinking of fresh oranges
the ones I picked today are still sour and green
I've made a note to send you a cartload
but not until frost covers the trees on Tungting

173

寓居永定精舍

政拙忻罷守　閑居初理生　家貧何由往　夢想在京城
野寺霜露月　晨興羈旅情　聊租二頃田　方課子弟耕
眼暗文字廢　身閑道心精　即與人羣遠　豈謂是非嬰

Written in the fall of 790 in Suchou. Wei apparently resigned his post as magistrate early enough in the year to plant a garden. Too poor or too ill to return home to Ch'ang-an, he moved to Yungting Temple in the countryside west of Suchou. According to researchers at the Suchou Museum, the temple and its grounds were located near what is now Suchou's West Garden Temple. Yungting Temple was later relocated just inside the city's southeast wall, but not while Wei Ying-wu was alive. In line six, I've used the variant *ch'en* (mornings) in place of *nung* (farmers). (8/7a)

Dwelling at Yungting Hermitage

An inept official I was happy to resign
but being retired means supporting myself
too poor to go anywhere else
I return to the capital in my dreams
in a country temple when the weather turns cold
mornings make me feel like traveling
meanwhile I've rented two hectares of land
and teach the children of farmers
my sight is so dim I can barely read
but I'm relaxed and focused on the Way
now that I'm living far from the crowd
why do right and wrong still find me

174

城中臥疾知閤薛二子屢從邑令
飲因以贈之

車馬日蕭蕭　胡不枉我廬　方來從令飲　臥病獨何如
秋風起江皋　開戶望平蕪　即此稀音素　焉知中密疎
渴者不思火　寒者不求水　人生羈寓時　去就當如此
猶希心異跡　眷眷存終始

Written in the fall of 790 in Suchou, shortly after he resigned his post as magistrate. Wei is living in his hut at Yungting Temple west of town — although he likes to think of it as still "in town" — along one of the canals that still run through the city. He is too ill to join his friends at a party held by the magistrate who replaced him and did not live to see another fall. (2/3b)

Lying Ill in Town, I Learn That My Two Friends, Yen and Hsueh, Have Been Drinking with the Magistrate and Accordingly Give Them This Poem

> All day I hear horses whinny
> why don't they stop at my hut
> you've come from drinking with the magistrate
> what can I do lying here ill
> autumn wind stirs along the waterside
> I open my door to a sea of rushes
> I never hear any news
> of things distant or even nearby
> someone who's thirsty doesn't long for fire
> someone who's cold doesn't look for water
> our lives are transient affairs
> thus do we come and go
> still our thoughts and deeds have rarely differed
> and our affection has remained unchanged

175

永定寺喜辟強夜至

子有新歲慶　獨此苦寒歸　夜叩竹林寺　山行雪滿衣

深爐正燃火　空齋共掩扉　還將一樽對　無言百事違

Written at the beginning of 791 at his hermitage outside Suchou. Chao Pi-ch'iang was one of Wei's nephews. With this Wei stopped writing poems. According to his epitaph, he died later that year in government lodging inside the city, although the exact date isn't given. (8/7a)

At Yungting Temple Pi-ch'iang Happily Arrives during the Night

> You came with New Year's greetings
> walking here alone in the bitter cold
> knocking on a bamboo temple gate at night
> covered with snow from your hike through the hills
> after starting a fire deep in my stove
> and closing the door to my empty room
> we shared a gourd full of wine
> and didn't speak of all the things that went wrong

Epitaphs

Epitaph of Wei Ying-wu's wife, Yuan P'ing, written by Wei Ying-wu upon her death in 776. It is the only known example of his handwriting. The dimensions of the original inscription are 18 × 17 inches.

唐故尚書左司郎中蘇州刺史京兆韋君墓誌銘並序

守尚書祠部員外郎騎都尉賜緋魚袋吳興丘丹纂

君諱應物，字義博，京兆杜陵人也。其先，高陽之孫，昌意之子，別封豕韋氏。漢初有韋孟者，孫賢，為鄒魯大儒，累遷，代蔡義為丞相。子玄成，學習父業，又代于定國為丞相。奕世繼位，家于杜陵。後十七代至逍遙公敻，枕跡丘園，周明帝屢降玄纁之禮，竟不能屈，以全黃綺之志。公弟郿公孝寬，名著周、隋，爵位崇顯，備於國史。逍遙公有子六人，俱為尚書。五子世沖，民部尚書、義豐公，則君之五代祖。皇刑部尚書，兼御史大夫、黃門侍郎、扶陽公挺(原文無此字，據《新唐書•宰相世系表》補)，君之高祖。皇尚書左仆射同中書門下三品待價，君(此字為抄者宙上下文意補，原文無)之曾祖。皇梁州都督令儀，君之烈祖。皇宣州司法參軍鑾，君之烈考。

君，司法之第三子也。門承台鼎，天資貞粹，丱角之年，已有不易之操。以蔭補右千牛，改左羽林倉曹，授高陵尉、廷評、洛陽丞、河南兵曹、京兆功曹。朝廷以京畿為四方政本，精選令長，除戶縣、櫟陽二縣令，遷比部郎。詔以滁人凋殘，領滁州刺史。負戴如歸，加朝散大夫，尋遷江州刺史。如滁上之政，時廉使有從權之斂，君以調非明詔，悉無所供。因有是非之訟，有司詳按，聖上以州疏端切，優詔賜封扶風縣開國男，食邑三百戶。征拜左司郎中，總轄六官，循舉戴、魏之法。尋領蘇州刺史，下車周星，豪猾屏息，方欲陟明，遇疾終乎官舍。池雁隨喪，州人罷市。素車一乘，旋於逍遙故園。茅宇竹亭，用設靈幾。歷官一十三政，三領大藩。儉德如此，豈不謂「貴而能貧者」矣！所著詩賦、議論、銘頌、記序，凡六百餘篇，行於當時。以貞元七年十一月八日，窆于少陵原，禮也。

夫人河南元氏，父挹，吏部員外郎。嘉姻柔則，君子是宜。先君即世，以龜筮不葉，未從合祔。以十二年十一月廿七日，嗣子慶複，啟舉有時，遂從夫人之禮。長女適大理評事楊凌。次女未笄，因父之喪，同月而逝。嗚呼！可謂孝矣！

余，吳士也，嘗忝州牧之舊，又辱詩人之目，登臨酬和，動盈卷軸。公詩原于曹、劉，參于鮑、謝。加以變態，意凌丹霄，忽造佳境，別開戶牖。惜夫位未崇年，不永而歿乎！泉局，哀哉！

堂弟端，河南府功曹，以儒孝承家，堂弟武，絳州刺史，以文學從政。慶複克荷遺訓，詞賦已工，鄉舉秀才，策居甲乙。泣血請銘，式昭幽壤。銘曰：

昌意本裔，豕韋別封。爰曆殷周，實逮勛庸。
漢曰孟賢，時致熙雍。泊乎逍遙，獨高其尚。
六子八座，五宗四相。流慶左司，帝貞貞亮。
作牧江水，政惟龔、黃。綱轄南宮，複舉舊章。
文變大雅，節貫秋霜。嗚呼彼蒼，殲我良牧。
禁掖方拜，寢門遄哭。見託篆銘，永志陵谷。

This is the text of Wei Ying-wu's epitaph written by his friend Ch'iu Tan. I have summarized its contents in the Preface.

About the Translator

Bill Porter assumes the pen name Red Pine for his translations. He was born in Los Angeles in 1943, grew up in the Idaho Panhandle, served a tour of duty in the U.S. Army (1964–67), graduated from the University of California with a degree in anthropology in 1970, and attended graduate school at Columbia University. Uninspired by the prospect of an academic career, he dropped out of Columbia in 1972 and moved to a Buddhist monastery in Taiwan. After four years with the monks and nuns, he struck out on his own and eventually found work at English-language radio stations in Taiwan and Hong Kong, where he produced over a thousand programs about his travels in China. In 1993 he returned to America with his family and has lived ever since in Port Townsend, Washington. His most recent publication is *Zen Baggage*, an account of a pilgrimage to sites associated with the beginning of Zen in China. He is currently working on a translation of the *Lankavatara Sutra*.

The Chinese character for poetry is made up of two parts: "word" and "temple" (or originally, as Red Pine notes, "from the heart"). It also serves as pressmark for Copper Canyon Press.

Since 1972, Copper Canyon Press has fostered the work of emerging, established, and world-renowned poets for an expanding audience. The Press thrives with the generous patronage of readers, writers, booksellers, librarians, teachers, students, and funders—everyone who shares the belief that poetry is vital to language and living.

Major funding has been provided by:

Anonymous

Janet and Leslie Cox

Beroz Ferrell & The Point, LLC

Cynthia Hartwig and Tom Booster

Lannan Foundation

National Endowment for the Arts

Cynthia Lovelace Sears and Frank Buxton

Washington State Arts Commission

For information and catalogs:

COPPER CANYON PRESS
Post Office Box 271
Port Townsend, Washington 98368
360-385-4925
www.coppercanyonpress.org

In Such Hard Times is set in MVB Verdigris, a text face by Mark van Bronkhorst, inspired by the sixteenth-century typefaces of Robert Granjon (roman) and Pierre Haultin (italic). The display type is Seria, by Martin Majoor. Book design by Valerie Brewster, Scribe Typography. Chinese typesetting by Pristine Communications in Taipei, Taiwan. Printed on archival-quality paper.

CPSIA information can be obtained
at www.ICGtesting.com
Printed in the USA
JSHW020439281221
21584JS00002B/4